The Yoga of Marketing

INDIGORIVER
PUBLISHING

The Yoga *of* Marketing

Balancing Heart, Mind, and Spirit for Success

JEANNA VALENTI

with Rachel Sacco

Introduction by Mariel Hemingway

The Yoga of Marketing: Balancing Heart, Mind, and Spirit for Success

Library of Congress Control Number: 2025919430
ISBN: 978-1-964686-83-7 (paperback) 978-1-964686-84-4 (ebook)

Editors: Jennifer Casey, Deborah Froese
Cover and Interior Design: Emma Elzinga

Printed in the United States of America

First Edition

3 West Garden Street, Ste. 718
Pensacola, FL 32502
www.indigoriverpublishing.com

Ordering Information:

Quantity sales: Special discounts are available on quantity purchases by corporations, associations, and others. For details, contact the publisher at the address above.

Orders by US trade bookstores and wholesalers: Please contact the publisher at the address above.

For Daniel

Contents

A Note from Mariel Hemingway

It is with great pleasure that I introduce Jeanna Valenti's inspiring work, The Yoga of Marketing: Balancing Heart, Mind, and Spirit for Success. From Jeanna's expertise as a Seven Spiritual Laws of Yoga teacher and insightful meditation and mindfulness instructor, this book offers a valuable perspective on the union of consciousness, mindfulness, and awareness and the business of marketing.

Whether you are an experienced or beginning yogini, a novice, or an experienced businessperson simply seeking a deeper understanding of yoga and marketing, this book provides a compelling and well-researched exploration.

– Mariel Hemingway

Birth of a Book

In July of 2013, I traveled to visit my dear friend Trudy Reeves, who lives in God's country—Monterey, California. Trudy and I met at a meditation retreat years prior at Esalen Institute, the holistic retreat and educational center tucked along the wild and majestic glittering coastline of Big Sur along California's enchanting Highway 1.

During our visit, we meditated and walked along the cliffs, mountainsides, and shimmering seacoasts of Carmel-by-the-Sea and Monterey. To say that I was awe-inspired would be an understatement. As a self-proclaimed personal growth and self-discovery retreat junkie, I felt I had landed in the most healing and inspiring spot on the planet. Nestled amongst the cypress and pine trees, I truly felt an awakening within.

And no mistake, as it is when nature speaks to me, that is precisely when a divinely inspired moment planted an idea in my mind's eye. I was going to write a book titled *The Yoga of Marketing*. The book would bridge the world of consciousness, mindfulness, and awareness with the world of business (or busyness) and marketing. In many ways, I envisioned the book uniting the left side of the brain (analytical and logical) and the right side of the brain (creative and spatial) so that readers could attain the perfect sense of balance between life and work that many of us aspire to. Stop with the human *doings* and get back to the human *beings*.

Once I thought it through, that spark of inspiration seemed absurd to my logical and practical left brain. I had a full-time and demanding executive marketing position in corporate America. I was busy raising my precious young toddler, and I knew nothing about what it would take to write a book.

I tucked the idea away for "when I had more time."

Fast forward three months. After I delivered a presentation on The Yoga of Marketing to a group of newly certified meditation instructors in Sedona, Arizona, Margaret Mills, a managing partner from IBM, approached me and asked me to co-author a book on the subject with her. I had just completed my Seven Spiritual Laws of Yoga training at the Deepak Chopra Center for Wellbeing, then located in Carlsbad, California. I began again to think in terms of a book that would weave my experience from a nearly thirty-year corporate marketing and public relations career with my love of yoga philosophy and practice to deliver a fresh, innovative, and contemporary approach to mindfulness and marketing.

Finally, more than ten years later, this book was born. The lessons found in *The Yoga of Marketing*, already tested on hundreds of people and companies (case studies included), are an inspiring guide to mindfulness and its capacity to positively influence marketing businesses, books, speakers, products, and services.

Yoga beautifully unites body, mind, and spirit for holistic health. The yoga philosophy and practice align us with our spirit or soul, which in turn aligns us with our desires and the desires of nature. We are already one with nature, and the practice of yoga philosophy helps us become more aware of this unity. Wellbeing emerges from this state of expanded awareness. Desires are effortlessly fulfilled.

From my earliest experience with the practice of yoga, I was completely captivated by its ability to heal the mind and body. The healing arts have enthralled me since I was seven years old. My mother suffered from severe and chronic back pain due to osteoarthritis, rheumatoid arthritis, and scoliosis, and I sought a cure for her because I wanted her to live a healthy, happy, and pain-free life. I wish I'd known about yoga then. I would have had her doing downward-facing dogs in the hills of beautiful Appalachia where I grew up.

Although I didn't know about yoga at that time, I did discover something that shared yoga's foundation in holistic health and wellbeing. After tearing a reflexology foot map from a women's health magazine, I patiently and thoroughly massaged my mom's feet. In reflexology, each part of the foot corresponds to a specific organ and system of the body. Pressure applied to the feet is believed to relax and heal the corresponding body area to relieve tension and treat illness. My dad was in on the healing action, too. He massaged the left side of Mom's spine so much that he wore a hole in her favorite *Be Kind* T-shirt.

Growing up so close to someone in chronic, debilitating pain eventually led me to yoga, where I discovered my way to peace of mind and body. It inspired my desire to help others find their way, too.

Yoga is becoming more mainstream. Organizations such as the United States military, the National Institutes of Health, and large corporations such as Apple, Nike, Google, and Forbes are listening to and incorporating scientific validation of the value of yoga, meditation, and mindfulness in health care. Many companies have incorporated yoga into their employee wellness and assistance programs for the physical and mental benefits the practice offers to employees, as well as its ability to boost motivation.

In addition to the physical poses most people associate with yoga, the holistic expression of the yoga philosophy connects the mind and body through various means, including conscious breathing techniques, meditation, wisdom, and lifestyle practices. All these methods connect the mind and body so individuals can realize their highest potential—in business and life. Embracing the practice of yoga unlocks full creative potential with grace and ease—or, as my friend Victoria calls it, *grace ease.*

Yoga improves strength, balance, and flexibility. It helps with back pain relief, eases arthritis symptoms, and benefits heart health. Needless to say, when we strengthen our bodies and minds through the practice of yoga or other healing modalities, all other aspects of our lives benefit as everything is interconnected. That includes marketing. Life is all energy and information in a dynamic state of fluctuation—expansion and contraction.

In ancient Chinese philosophy, the Yin and Yang concept describes how seemingly opposite forces may be interdependent and interconnected. With Yin being the receptive or feminine force and Yang the active masculine movement, the two halves together complete wholeness. So it is with *The Yoga of Marketing.* The process naturally flows and changes with time. Typical marketing pushes, such as email blasts and outreaches to a company's database, must be balanced with periods of silence and inquiry.

Word-of-mouth marketing must be balanced with content marketing and social media messaging. From unique differentiators and value propositions to distinct brand images and messages, I guide readers to the most important elements for themselves, their brands, and their businesses.

If there's one thing I've learned in my thirty years of being a marketing and public relations consultant, twenty of them spent helping authors, it's that most businesspeople dislike marketing. Authors love to write books, business owners love to create and run businesses, and program developers love to offer their programs and products. But very few love to market. And if they don't flat-out hate it, they shy away from marketing because they don't know how to do it, they think it is sales-y, or they don't want to "bother" people.

Complaints range from "I'm not very good at putting myself out there" to "I just don't know what to do." Of course, hiring someone like me is a solution, but not everyone's budget allows room to hire a professional marketing or public relations consultant. Unfortunately, ineffective marketing—or none at all—is the downfall of many enterprises that would otherwise be moderately or even highly successful.

Even though most people do not like to market, there is a way to become mindful, conscious, and aware and use that space to create a meaningful marketing approach that does not induce stress or frustration.

Imagine this. You just finished writing the marketing plan to launch your new product, book, or service, and you enjoyed every minute of the process. You're relaxed and happy, confident that you're presenting yourself and your project authentically—and in a way that will attract new clients and help your business grow. You are energized and excited to implement your plan. You are motivated to succeed. In fact, you can hardly wait to get going!

Does this seem realistic to you? For most people, marketing is worse than pulling teeth—but it doesn't have to be. *The Yoga of Marketing* offers a different way.

After an introduction to the ancient disciplines of yoga and the three yogic practices we will draw upon here (chakras, breathwork, and meditation), we'll take a deeper look at each chakra and then at seven corresponding marketing centers with stories from some of my clients who have experienced success with *The Yoga of Marketing* process.

We'll also explore how your practice of yoga spills over into life and leadership. My friend Rachel Sacco, President and CEO of Experience Scottsdale, the most heart-centered leader I know, contributed Chapter Four, "The Yoga of Leadership."

The Yoga of Marketing shares mindfulness techniques, yoga, and meditation exercises that align with decades of marketing expertise to help businesses and authors succeed. These practices teach us how to be present in each moment. You'll find plenty of resources to support your practices at www.theyogaofmarketing.com/bonuses.

Just as practicing yoga regularly is the only way to improve, so is marketing. Consistency is key. Every marketer knows their role is not a "one-and-done" kind of thing. Marketers need to consistently create content, craft brands, and develop authentic relationships by engaging with clients and customers on a regular basis. There are no shortcuts.

Yoga reminds us that starting small ensures whatever we do is done with excellence. The same goes for marketing. Value quality over quantity and build from there. My time-tested formula for heart and soul marketing success is the solution to your marketing woes. Whether you're a visionary CEO, a creative entrepreneur, a novice, or a lifelong devoted yogini, *The Yoga of Marketing* brings solid tools and principles to develop a mindfulness or meditation practice that will help grow a business and better market goods and services. The guide helps readers stay personally strong and motivated without despair and distraction, focusing on sound, mindful marketing principles and fusing them with deeply internal yoga methods.

My hope is that heart-centered entrepreneurs, businesses—and authors especially—will appreciate the new vantage point of energetic, mind-body, compassionate, and mindful marketing approaches and techniques. Gone is the old paradigm of "push, push, sell, sell" and overkill in email blasts, something consumers are tired of seeing. We've long needed a new paradigm of marketing, one that includes caring, service, kindness, and authenticity. The nuggets and wisdom in this book teach those who are hungry for this how to do it. For additional support, Appendix A addresses a timeline and marketing strategies for launching a new product or service. Appendix B offers several author-related resources drawn from my years of experience with the publication industry.

In a noisy world of frenetic social media tweets, fake news, email bombardment, and overcrowded inboxes, *The Yoga of Marketing* offers mindful solutions for busy professionals who can be easily distracted by the hyperactive and often interruptive digital media. By implementing the techniques and practices in the book, individuals and companies will create name recognition and brand awareness for their products and services, develop thought leadership status, and attract customers for life. *The Yoga of Marketing* is a comprehensive and mindful guide to fixing the marketing problem with a sustainable solution.

As the wise mystic poet Jalal al-Din Muhammad Rumi said, "When you do things from your soul, you feel a river moving in you, a joy."

As you flow through these pages and practice the exercises, may you feel inspired and empowered while fostering peace, love, inspiration, healing, and connection to both marketing and your individual self.

As always, please confer with your doctor before taking part in any physical yoga practice.

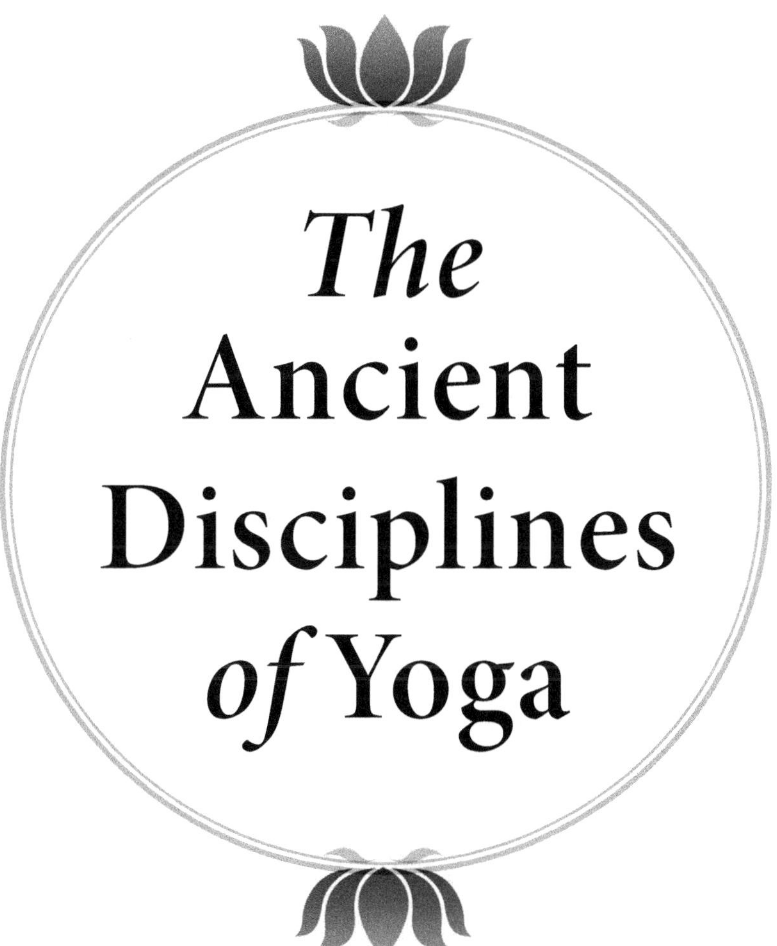

The Ancient Disciplines *of* Yoga

The word yoga *is derived from the Sanskrit root* yuj, *meaning "to yoke" or "to unite." This five-thousand-year-old practice, which includes movement, breathing techniques, meditation, and an awareness of the body's chakra (energy) system, aims to create a union between body, mind, and spirit, as well as between the individual self and universal consciousness. It seems to me that everything a person does comes together more effectively when the body, mind, and spirit are in alignment.*

1

Yoga Concepts

I've been asked if yoga is an exercise or even a religion. Despite misconceptions about what yoga actually is, most teachers tend to agree that the yoga philosophy aims to deliver liberation from suffering. Some yoga experts claim that yoga is a physical, mental, and spiritual system for living in harmony with the universe.

Over thousands of years of practice, many different styles of yoga have emerged. Styles combine physical postures, breathing techniques, and meditation in various ways. Modern yoga is most often associated with the physical practice of asanas (poses and postures), which aim to achieve balance, flexibility, and strength in the body. However, the physical aspect reflects only one small part of the tradition and ancient philosophy of yoga. Yoga practice also nurtures the mind and spirit.

The Yoga of Marketing focuses on the mind and spirit. While the book refers to various asanas (poses and postures), it pays particular attention to the chakra system and managing your internal energy and breathwork. Through meditation, we learn to balance that energy and deepen our connection with self to raise self-awareness and expand consciousness, the primary force in the universe. The practices we will explore help bring calm and a sense of peace to a world that is often chaotic and tangled in challenge.

As a certified mindfulness and meditation instructor with a deep appreciation for all aspects of yoga, including the chakra system, I have several techniques to offer and help you expand your experience.

Chakras

Whenever I lead a chakra toning exercise in a yoga class or retreat, my students report feeling more alive, vibrant, and joyful. Out of all the healing modalities offered, chakra balancing has been their favorite. So, I decided to focus on a deeper understanding of the chakras and how they can help us heal and thrive.

I find the chakras truly fascinating. They can be understood as vortexes of energy that also act as clearing houses for negative energy. We create energy in them, process energy in them, and process information that comes into our consciousness or energetic field, also known by some as our *auric field* or *electromagnetic field.* Many believe this field extends about two feet beyond the body. My friend's husband, Marty, calls it "the field of love." We can transform and transmute the energy within our chakras to become more balanced human beings.

The chakra system originated in India between 1500 and 500 BC. It first appeared in the Vedas, the most ancient scriptures of Hinduism. The word *chakra* comes from the ancient Sanskrit language and translates to "wheel" or "disk." As you now know, the chakras represent various energy centers in the body, which are associated with specific nerve bundles and internal organs. If these energy centers are well-maintained and aligned, we experience excellent health and wellbeing. Life and work flow effortlessly. But if these energy centers become blocked, we may begin to experience physical or emotional symptoms. That can lead to disease—and *dis*-ease—disrupting life and work. So, balancing the chakras maintains the free flow of energy in our bodies, which explains the translation of the chakra as a "wheel" or "cycle."

Although the body has more than a hundred chakras, when we talk about chakras, we are usually referring to the seven main energy centers that run from the base of the spinal cord to just above the top of the head. In yogic philosophy, chakras are influenced by emotions and thought and also by color, food, essential oils, crystals, yoga poses, mantras, and even music, which is why singing bowls of various pitches are so popular during yoga classes.

Did you know that each of the seven notes in the major diatonic scale aligns with one of the seven main chakras? When a note from this scale is produced, it activates the corresponding chakra, which then sends the energy or aura from that chakra to the physical body.

The Hindus call this subtle energy *prana*; the Chinese call it *chi*, and the Japanese call it *ki*. When you want to enhance certain energies, find the corresponding note with a tuner or instrument. Hum or listen to that note while visualizing the part of the body where that chakra or energy center is located. Some practitioners use crystal bowls and other methods, like gongs, to create the specific tones and vibrations that you need. I like to listen to the 852 Hz frequency on YouTube. It's known as the "frequency of love."

We'll discuss each chakra in Chapter Two more, but for now, notice how they are situated along the spine from the tailbone to the top of the head. Each is assigned a color ranging from red (at the base of the spine) to white, violet, or an iridescent color (at the crown).

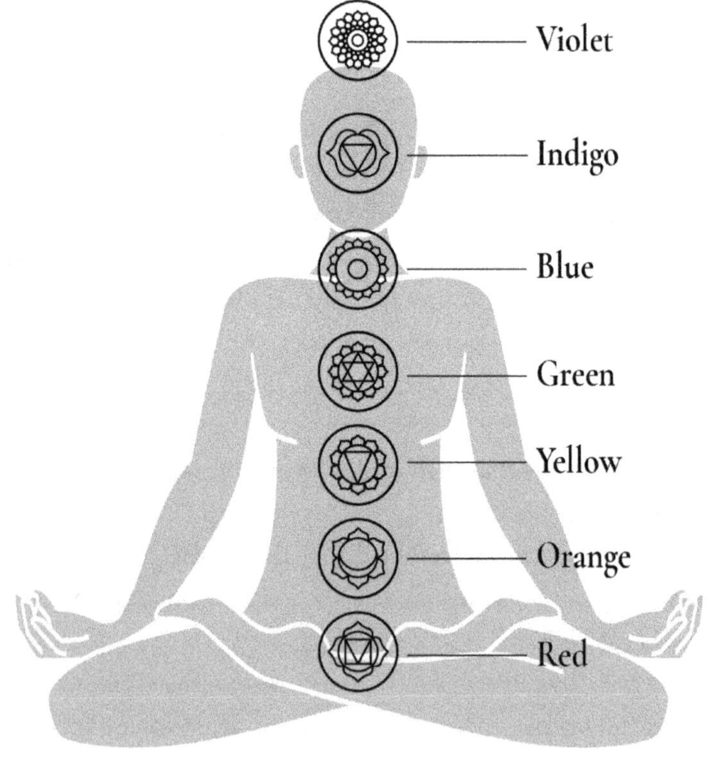

Utilizing the specific elements associated with a chakra activates that chakra. Over time, with care and attention, each chakra's qualities will grow more apparent in your life and your work.

Breathwork

Breathing is incredibly important. If we're breathing deeply, we are vitally alive. Yet, how many of us actually practice breathing consciously as if our lives depend on it?

Smooth and steady breathing that is evenly balanced in length and application is nourishing not only to our nervous systems but to every single cell in our bodies. I've heard the expression numerous times in my yoga community: "Conscious breathing equals a conscious life." Some of my yogini friends say that we do not actually breathe; instead, we are *being* breathed.

According to the yoga tradition, *prana* (breath, life force energy) rules over the five senses and the entire body. Prana allows us to experience life. So in yoga traditions, it's said that if a part of the body is not functioning well, it is likely deficient in prana. When we begin a yoga practice, one of the first lessons we learn is to breathe in and out through the nose. Breathing through the mouth is inherently shallow, almost sharp, and thus has more of an aggressive effect on the nervous system. Nasal breathing triggers greater use of the diaphragm and invites a deeper breath, which gets more oxygen into the system. If yoga means union, then we want to focus on the union of linking mind, body, and breath along with mind, body, and spirit.

But where do we begin? How can we consciously work with the breath in a way that creates balance and keeps us calm and centered? We can create harmony in body, breath, and mind by simply focusing our attention on the practice of taking long, slow, deep breaths to bring us into the present moment. Let's give it a try. Softly close your eyes and take a few long, slow, deep breaths in and out for the next few minutes.

Meditation

Meditation is a vital part of yoga. During a meditation practice, we quiet the mind, focus on the present moment, and explore the present moment as it is without attaching to our thoughts. In other words, when we're meditating, we engage in contemplation or reflection.

There are many ways to practice meditation. Whether you choose to let your thoughts go, focus on a mantra, or practice visualization, meditation creates room to reflect or release, clearing away the information overload that builds every day and contributes to our stress levels. An online search will reveal an endless array of approaches to meditation that may invite you to sit, stand, walk, or engage in some other form of movement to meditate.

The Mayo Clinic has pinpointed specific proven emotional and physical benefits of meditation, including:

- Gaining a new perspective on stressful situations
- Building skills to manage our stress
- Increasing self-awareness
- Focusing on the present
- Reducing negative emotions
- Increasing imagination and creativity
- Increasing patience and tolerance

- Lowering resting heart rate
- Lowering resting blood pressure
- Improving sleep quality[1]

Let's take a look at the three types of meditation that we'll use in this book.

Mantra Meditation

A mantra, also known as an instrument of the mind, is a syllable, word, or phrase repeated during meditation.

The word "mantra" comes from a Sanskrit word meaning "a sacred sound, message, or text." Mantras may be a collection of sounds or may include words that have a literal meaning. They can be chanted, spoken, or whispered repeatedly, spoken aloud or silently in the mind. A seed mantra consists of a single syllable or word. (In the next chapter, you'll find a specific seed mantra to enliven each chakra.)

A mantra is a tool for releasing the mind from its constant barrage of thoughts. It helps us concentrate, settle down, and get in the right calm frame of mind for meditation. Many people find that using a mantra can boost awareness and improve concentration. Research shows that mantras act as tools to ease the mind and release worrisome thoughts.

If you have a mantra specifically selected for you by a certified meditation instructor, you may choose to repeat that mantra. If not, silently repeat a Sanskrit mantra for the mindful meditation exercise below.

---

1 "Meditation: A Simple, Fast Way to Reduce Stress," Mayo Clinic, December 14, 2023, https://www.mayoclinic.org/tests-procedures/meditation/in-depth/meditation/art-20045858

A simple mantra you can use for this mindful meditation is *OM Shanti Shanti Shanti.* Like many mantras, this one begins with the sound *OM*. The sound *OM* holds no specific meaning, but it is the primordial sound, the sound of the universe, or the sound from which all other sounds are derived and formed.

The Sanskrit word *Shanti* means peace. *OM Shanti Shanti Shanti* is a powerful, energetic Vedic mantra or sacred sound with healing vibrations that is considered to call forth cosmic peace. It is chanted for peace in the body, mind, and spirit.

Repeat your mantra silently with your eyes closed for ten minutes until your timer goes off. If your mind begins to wander during the meditation, simply bring your attention back to the mantra. Go easy on yourself. If you hear noises or become distracted during the meditation, simply bring your attention gently back to the mantra.

Mindful Meditation

Mindful meditation is a mental training practice that teaches us to slow down racing thoughts, let go of negativity, and calm the mind and body.

Find a quiet spot where you can remain undisturbed for ten minutes. Dress comfortably and sit upright with your spine straight and relaxed and your head up. If you'd like, place a blanket around your shoulders for comfort and warmth in case you get chilly. If desired, prop up your arms and legs with pillows.

I coach my yoga students to imagine a thin golden thread going from the top of their heads up toward the heavens. Tuck your stomach in and lift your shoulders back and down so that your spine is straight and you are sitting comfortably upright.

Set an alarm clock, egg timer, or your phone alarm for ten minutes. If possible, make the alarm chime sound soothing so that the noise is not too jarring when you emerge from your meditation practice. Many vendors sell meditation timers specifically designed for meditation.

Close your eyes and breathe slowly, deeply, and consciously. If you have a mantra, a word or sound repeated to aid concentration in meditation that a professional meditation instructor has given you, silently repeat that mantra over the course of the next ten minutes.

Once your timer goes off, slowly wiggle your fingers and toes, and gently begin to ease back into gentle movement. Slowly open your eyes and bring your attention back to the present moment. Notice how you feel.

Chakra Meditation

Chakra meditations help us improve focus and concentration. Focusing on our chakras allows us to grow more in tune with body and mind, leading to improved physical and mental health. This form of meditation can also help reduce stress and anxiety and create a feeling of wellbeing and calmness.

To begin a chakra meditation, find a peaceful place where you won't be interrupted for twenty minutes to half an hour. Sit in a comfortable position with your spine straight, not rigid, with your legs folded in front of you. You can sit on a cushion or pillow if you find the position uncomfortable. Let your hands fall limp on your knees. Start to focus on each part of your body, starting with your feet and working your way up to the top of your head. As you do this, focus on having each part of your body relax. The goal is to melt away any stress or tension you may feel in the body.

The next step in the chakra meditation process is to focus on the breath. Gently allow the breath to become steady and deep. If your mind starts to wander, gently bring your attention back to the breath and continue to focus on each inhale and exhale that you take.

Begin to visualize each chakra running from the root at the base of your spine to the crown chakra located just above your head. As you do, envision the energy flowing into and through each chakra. Put your attention on each chakra and begin to enliven that area of your body. First, focus on the root chakra (base of spine). Move to the sacral chakra (just below the navel). Follow that with the solar plexus chakra (stomach), the heart chakra (center of chest), the throat chakra (base of throat toward the spine), the third eye chakra (between the brows), and the crown chakra (just above the top of the head).

In my own yoga practice, I like to chant a mantra for each chakra at the top of my lungs. Students from my classes and retreats have shown a deep appreciation for this practice, which helps relieve stress and shed negative energy stored in their bodies. We chant, sing, or hum each mantra as we visualize the vibrant colors associated with each chakra. Each mantra's vibration resonates with the chakra to enliven and heal every single cell in our bodies.

You'll find mantras specific to each chakra in Chapter Two. On my website, www.theyogaofmarketing.com/bonuses, you'll find an audio recording of this exercise.

❊

If you are new to meditation, do not worry if your mind begins to wander or if you fall asleep during your meditation practice. This is normal and expected. The best meditation practice is the one that you will actually do on a regular basis. Stick with the practice. When your mind begins to wander—and it will—simply and gently bring your attention back to your mantra or the focal point of your meditation. Over time, your meditation practice can reap a plethora of benefits, including stress reduction, reducing negative emotions and promoting emotional health, controlling anxiety, kindness generation, sleep improvement, pain control, decrease in blood pressure, increases in patience and tolerance, lengthened attention span, and enhanced self-awareness.

Certified meditation teachers recommend that students meditate twice daily for twenty minutes per session. It is completely fine to gradually ease into and work up to the twenty-minute sessions, perhaps starting with one or two minutes at a time. One of my meditation instructor's frequent reminders to her students is RPM: Rise. Pee. Meditate. She also encourages a second meditation in the late afternoon when stress levels tend to be high and blood pressure typically tends to be higher. Around three or four o'clock in the afternoon works well for the second meditation of the day, or when you can fit the quiet time into your schedule in the late afternoon or after work and before dinner.

According to research from the Harvard Business Review, even ten minutes of meditation daily can increase creativity.[2] Mindfulness meditation is becoming more mainstream. Many corporations, including Google, Goldman Sachs, General Mills,

---

2 Emma Schootstra, Dirk Deichmann, and Evgenia Dolgova, "Can 10 Minutes of Meditation Make You More Creative?" Harvard Business Review, August 29, 2017, https://hbr.org/2017/08/can-10-minutes-of-meditation-make-you-more-creative.

SAP, Intel, Ernst & Young, Forbes, and others, now have meditation and mindfulness departments. They put practices in place to help their employees reduce stress, enhance their creativity, and spark innovative thoughts. Far from viewing meditation practices as "hippie dippy woo-woo," companies like the Mayo Clinic, Nike, Apple, AstraZeneca, and Aetna are singing meditation's praises (or, in some cases, chanting its *OMs*).

What was once an ancient practice has now made its way into the mainstream fabric of American culture. According to an article in *The Harvard Gazette,* NASA research shows that those who meditate have larger brains than those who do not meditate. NASA says that meditation helps improve concentration and focus, which certainly can help people use their brains. NASA's Langley Research Center suggests that meditation improves spontaneous creativity.[3]

My meditation instructor, Sarah McLean, founder of the McLean Meditation Institute, suggests that the way we treat ourselves in our meditation is the way we treat ourselves as we live our lives. Here, in summary, are the five essentials to meditation success found in her book, *Soul-Centered: Transform Your Life in 8 Weeks with Meditation.*[4]

1. **It's Okay to Have Thoughts**. You do not need to stop thinking completely while in meditation. Instead, your meditation practice will naturally settle down your mind, body, and nervous system, making it easier to quiet the mind and meditate.

---

3 William J. Cromie, "Meditation found to increase brain size," T*he Harvard Gazette,* February 2, 2006, https://news.harvard.edu/gazette/story/2006/02/meditation-found-to-increase-brain-size/.

4 Sarah McLean, Transform Your Life in 8 Weeks with Meditation (Hay House, 2012), pp. xxii-xxv.

2. **Don't Try Too Hard.** At first, you may try to do it "right." But you'll soon find that overworking it, trying too hard, forcing it, or concentrating only creates more thoughts and bad habits.

3. **Let Go of Expectations.** You may have preconceived notions about what is supposed to happen during meditation and how you should feel or experience it. Let that all go.

4. **Be Kind to Yourself.** An essential key to meditating correctly is being kind to yourself. You'll begin to notice that how you treat yourself in meditation is how you treat yourself in life. If your mind wanders, you fall asleep, or you get lost in yourself, be kind and gentle with yourself and go right back to the focus of your meditation, which may be a mantra.

5. **Stick with It.** Finally, meditation only works if you stick with it and don't give up. By staying with the practice, you will create a new relationship with your mind.

Now, let's explore how these essential elements of yoga can help you engage with life and marketing in an entirely new way.

2

The Chakras

We all have seven major chakras or energy centers. Each center corresponds to specific nerve bundles and internal organs, providing subtle energy to help the mind, body, organs, and intellect work at optimum levels. These centers impact us physically, psychologically, and spiritually.

You've probably heard people talk about "unblocking" their chakras. When chakras are unblocked, they're open. Energy runs through them freely, and that creates harmony among the physical body, mind, and spirit.

Each chakra expresses a different aspect of the personality. Assessing the chakras provides a lot of information about an individual's life story. That story includes information about how someone feels, how they behave, where they are stuck in life, their strengths, their weaknesses, and even insights into past experiences.

All these insights are powerful tools for improving our lives.

Root Chakra: Foundation

sthair·ya: stability

Everything needs a strong foundation—from the one supporting your home or business to the roots nourishing a tree and the shoes stabilizing your feet. And so, we begin our journey with the root chakra, the chakra grounding body, mind, and spirit.

As noted previously, the first chakra is located at the base of the spine. Also known as the *Muladhara* chakra, Sanskrit for "the basis of existence," the root chakra represents the earth element, grounding us and providing the support and foundation we require to live life fully. As the first energy center, it is associated with awareness of the physical body and the primal, animal nature of survival. It must be balanced for us to feel safe, secure, and at home in our bodies and in our lives.

If you suffer from extended stress, which can create adrenal problems, balancing your root chakra may help, as it governs the adrenal glands. When the root chakra is strong and functioning well, you can release stress from your nervous system and live in the present moment.

Yoga practice emphasizes the root chakra to ensure a stable foundation and core. Once strength is attained, flexibility and balance can grow.

The root chakra houses a powerful form of energy called kundalini. This energy is the source of life force, also known as prana or chi. Yogic science teaches that this energy coils like a serpent, three-and-a-half times over around the base of the spine. When dormant kundalini energy is activated or awakened, we can access our highest potential in every area of life.

Think of *strength* and *survival* when you think of the root chakra energy center.

Balance Your Root Chakra

There are many ways to balance or tone the root chakra and reap rewards in every area of life—including marketing. Simple practices such as walking in nature or gardening are usually the most powerful. Recently, a big movement called "grounding" or "earthing" has been popularized. Using this therapeutic technique, individuals connect with the earth's surface and its natural electrical charge by walking barefoot on grass, sand, or soil or using grounding devices that connect to the ground port of an electrical outlet. Meditation, visualization, and healing modalities using color, scent, and crystals can also be helpful in balancing the root chakra.

Essential Tips

1. Visualize the root chakra as red. Red is the slowest of all wavelengths within the visible color spectrum and the most stimulating. It symbolizes energy, confidence, courage, and change.
2. The root chakra resonates with the C note. Yogis believe that the root chakra vibrates somewhere between 396 and 432 Hz. This frequency is thought to rid trauma, fear, and guilt.
3. The seed mantra for root chakra meditation is LAM, which means *I am*. Singing, chanting, or humming LAM grounds the root chakra and increases vitality, courage, and self-confidence.
4. For affirmation outside of meditation, repeat the phrase, "I am confident" or "I am healthy and vibrant."

5. The root chakra thrives on red foods that generate stability and self-awareness, such as tomatoes, strawberries, raspberries, cherries, red apples, peppers, and pomegranates. Root vegetables such as sweet potatoes, carrots, turnips, beets, garlic, parsnips, onions, rutabaga, and horseradish are helpful as well. Consider eggs, beans, nuts, and lean meat for protein, as well as ginger, turmeric, paprika, and cayenne for flavoring.
6. The yoga asanas (poses) that encourage root chakra balance include warrior one, easy pose, child's pose, and garland pose.
7. For advanced energetic healing, consider using the essential oils of tea tree, cinnamon, and cedarwood or crystals of red asper obsidian and hematite, which are known to balance the root chakra.

Mindfulness Meditation

To cultivate a sense of earthiness, stability, and vibrancy that nurtures your root chakra, here's a short mindfulness walking meditation you can practice at home or in a local garden.

Find a quiet spot outside, preferably in a grassy area. Take off your shoes. As you feel the ground beneath your feet, you begin to learn about the earth, known as Gaia in Greek, the primary quality of the *Muladhara* chakra. If you live in a cooler climate, consider layering your clothing and stepping outside to stand in the sunshine for a few minutes every day.

With your eyes half open, fix your gaze on the ground about two feet in front of your feet. Hold your left hand on top of your right hand near your waist with palms facing upward. Begin to take very slow, long steps walking in a circle or straight line.

Become totally mindful and aware of each step you take. Notice your entire body as it becomes involved in the action. Watch how each knee bends, lifts, and then straightens. Become aware of the movement of your ankles, hips, spine, and shoulders.

Keep bringing your gentle attention back to the soles of your feet and their interaction with the earth. Give your full and undivided attention to your movement.

Tune each step to your breath. Inhale as you very slowly lift your foot. Move your foot forward no more than three to four inches, and exhale as you lower your foot to the ground. As each foot touches the ground, feel it rooting itself deeply into the earth.

Take several deep breaths and return your gentle attention to your everyday activities. Notice how you feel.

Sacral Chakra: Creation

rach·nat·mak: great creativity

The second chakra, known in Sanskrit as the *Svadhisthana* chakra, is located in the pelvic area and the middle region of the lower back. It is associated with the gonads. *Svadhisthana* is the Sanskrit word for "dwelling place of the Self." Symbolized by the water element, *Svadhisthana* is all about flow, flexibility, and freedom of expression. Governed by the liquid elements of the body, including blood and lymph, this chakra is responsible for maintaining our body's fluid levels.

From a spiritual perspective, the sacral chakra is associated with creative instincts, our ability to relate to the world, and nurturing healthy relationships. It represents new beginnings, the birth of opportunity, and our creative powers. When we have healthy sacral chakra energy, creative juices flow effortlessly. When the sacral chakra is blocked or disordered, we become fearful of moving forward or taking risks. That leaves us feeling stuck, limited, and unable to birth new ideas or move in new directions.

Balance Your Sacral Chakra

If you'd like to balance or open the sacral chakra, bring either hand to this chakra's location, a few inches below the navel. Breathe in deeply, and then let out a long and slow chant, song, or hum of the mantra *VAM*. Send loving energy to this area of your body as you visualize it pulsing with a warm orange glow.

Because the second chakra is represented by the water element, any form of deep hydration will be beneficial, from drinking water to swimming in a natural body of water. Other ways to balance the sacral chakra include meditation or yoga, repeating positive affirmations and reflecting in solitude and nature.

Essential Tips

1. Visualize the sacral chakra as a vibrant, fiery orange. Orange symbolizes sacredness, fire, purity, warmth, enthusiasm, and excitement. This chakra is directed by the pleasure principle, and its main theme is to live life to the fullest. It promotes personal growth and the evolution of our personal identities.

2. The musical note D resonates with the second chakra. The frequency most associated with the sacral chakra, 417 Hz, is thought to alleviate stress and tension.
3. Yogis believe singing, chanting, or humming the seed mantra, VAM, cleanses and heals the sacral chakra center physically, emotionally, and spiritually.
4. The affirmation for the second chakra is "I feel."
5. Orange foods nourish, balance, and open the second chakra. Consider eating deep orange fruits and vegetables such as sweet potatoes, tangerines, and citrus fruits, including oranges and grapefruits. Other fruits such as mangoes, apricots, and peaches nourish this chakra, along with vegetables like squash, yams, and pumpkins. Nuts such as almonds, sesame, flax, and walnuts are sattvic and nourishing (light, good, pure). Foods rich in Omega-3s, like salmon, also work well. Coconut, spices, and cinnamon balance and strengthen the second chakra.
6. The yoga asanas (poses) known to open and balance the second chakra include bound angle pose and goddess pose. If you'd like to try a yoga pose to support balancing and opening your second chakra, consider cat-cow stretches. They are one of the best yoga poses to strengthen the back.
    - Move onto your hands and knees with your hands just under your shoulders and your knees right under your hips.
    - As you inhale, drop your belly down. As you exhale, round your spine, reversing the flow.

- While on your hands and knees, lift your pelvis up like a cow as you inhale and exhale deeply, bringing your head and pelvis down like a cat.
- Gently begin to circle your hips. Continue moving with your breath as you inhale and exhale. You can begin to make some big hip circles here as well, circling the hips back to the heels.

Opening the lower back and spine will allow more energy to flow to your sacral chakra. Yogis believe that the longevity of our lives is tied to the flexibility of our spines.

7. Orange and tangerine essential oils, as well as calcite and carnelian crystals, are known to heal and balance the second chakra.

Svadhisthana Meditation

Find a quiet, comfortable spot to sit. Then, with your sitting bones firmly planted on a chair or cushion or on the floor, keep your spine straight. Make sure that your head is parallel to the ceiling. Close your eyes, cross your legs, and place your hands on your thighs or in your lap with your hands in a water mudra.

Many asanas activate the *Svadhisthana* chakra. For this exercise, we'll use Sukhasana, a simple sitting pose.

Mudras are hand gestures practiced using the thumb and little finger. They help connect the brain to the body, soothe pain, stimulate endorphins, change moods, and increase vitality. The little finger represents the water element, which balances the water element in the body.

Sukhasana Pose

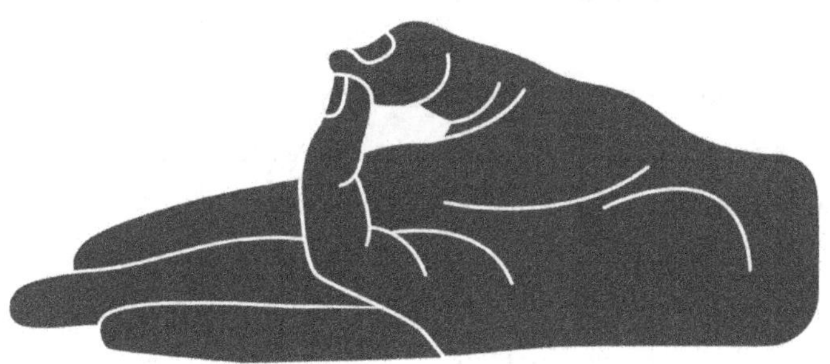

Water Mudra

So, for this exercise, please focus your attention on relaxing the entire body.

Allow your awareness to move away from your thoughts and drop deep down into your stomach. Allow your entire body to relax by noticing each body part, from your scalp to your toes. Relax all the muscles in your face. Take a deep breath in, and on the exhale, let go of everything you have been holding onto.

Begin to observe the natural rhythm of your own breathing. As my meditation teacher says, "What you put your attention on grows in your awareness," so if thoughts come, or if any sounds inside or outside your body capture your attention, notice them and let them go. Let them float across your mind like clouds float across the sky and return to your deep, conscious breathing. Breathe in and breathe out. As your breath becomes calmer, so will your mind.

Relax your neck, shoulders, arms, hands, belly, torso, hips, thighs, calves, ankles, and even your toenails. Place your awareness on your sacral chakra, located in your pelvic area, and envision a vibrant orange radiating from it as you continue to take deep, nourishing breaths. Sit as still as you can while holding this posture.

Continue to observe the breath for a few moments. Envision your orange chakra color glowing, growing, and expanding. Notice how it responds and how you respond. Relax for several breaths and simply notice.

When you feel completely relaxed, gradually open your eyes and notice how your body feels.

Solar Plexus Chakra: Power

shak·thi: ability, power

The third chakra, located in the solar plexus or stomach area, is known as the solar plexus or *Manipura* chakra in Sanskrit. The word "Manipura" means "lustrous gem of the city." Its vibrant yellow color is associated with the fire element and the sun. Physically, the third chakra is associated with the liver, spleen, and gallbladder. Spiritually, it connects with sight and one's sense of personal power, self-esteem, and reliability, governing our desires, intentions, will, and destiny—our ambitions and actions. When properly balanced, this chakra stimulates growth.

Balance Your Solar Plexus Chakra

There are many ways to balance or tone the solar plexus chakra. Asanas that twist the torso allow movement through the solar plexus energy center and help create balance. Working with the fire and sun elements that govern the third chakra also helps establish balance, so candle gazing is an effective form of meditation. The practice is as simple as it sounds. Stare at a candle flame and keep your attention and focus there.

Connect with the sun, too. The sun is associated with the masculine energy of the solar plexus. Wear yellow. The colors of the chakras follow the sequence of a rainbow—ROYGBIV, just like we learned in kindergarten. Moving from the root chakra to the higher chakras, each color increases in frequency.

Essential Tips

1. Infuse your thoughts about the solar plexus chakra with vibrant yellow, which relates to the fire element. This color symbolizes energy, intellect, and the connection we have with fire and the sun. It aligns with the third chakra's representation of youth, new beginnings, and rebirth.
2. The solar plexus chakra resonates with the E note. The E note vibrates at about 528 Hz, a frequency responsible for miracles and dramatic changes.
3. Singing, chanting, or humming RAM, the solar plexus seed mantra, stimulates third chakra energy. Vocalize the mantra aloud, and you will feel the sound vibrations resonate within your body. Repeat the mantra as many times as your intuition leads you to.
4. The positive affirmation associated with the third chakra is "I can."
5. Think of foods that match the chakra's vibrant yellow color—bananas, corn, lemons, pineapples, yellow curry, and so on. These foods nourish and support this chakra. It also thrives on foods such as oats, brown rice, spelt, beans, rye, farro, vegetables, and sprouted grains—all foods that provide crucial fiber and sustainable energy.
6. Asanas thought to balance the solar plexus chakra are boat pose, downward dog, and child's pose. Spinal twist and supine spinal twist are also helpful to move stomach area energy.
7. Essential oils, including lemon, lemongrass, and basil, are known to heal and balance the third chakra. Several

crystals can help, too: citrine, yellow tourmaline, yellow topaz, yellow tiger's eye, sunstone, yellow aventurine, peridot, yellow apatite, lemon quartz, and yellow jasper.

Soham, Sohum, or So Hum Meditation

Sit quietly on the ground or floor with your legs crossed comfortably. Feel your sitting bones rooted solidly in the ground or floor. Make sure your spine is comfortably straight and your head is parallel to the ceiling. (I like to envision a thin golden thread going from the top of my head up to the sky or heaven.) Lengthen your neck and begin to take several deep inhales and long exhales.

Set a timer for ten minutes.

Close your eyes and bring your hands into a prayer position around the heart chakra. As you breathe in, silently sing, chant, hum, imagine, or think the sound "So," and as you breathe out, silently sing, chant, hum, imagine, or think the sound "Hum" or "Ham." Repeat this process several times. With each inhale, notice your jaw softening and your entire body beginning to relax.

Continue to breathe slowly and align your mantra to your breath. Be careful not to rush your breath if you notice yourself speeding up your mantra.

Each time you notice your mind begin to wander—and it usually will—gently draw your attention back to your silent or spoken mantra. Align the pace of your mantra to the pace of your breath.

When your timer goes off, gently release your mantra and bring your attention back to your breath. Sit quietly for a minute or two before you open your eyes.

You have just completed one of the simplest yet most sacred mantras, which means, "I Am That I Am." As you repeat the So Hum mantra, you begin drawing your awareness to who you really are, the sacred soul and spiritual essence residing inside and around your body.

Heart Chakra: Spirit

sne·ha: to love

Known in Sanskrit as the *Anahata* chakra, the fourth chakra is located within the area of the heart and is associated with the thymus gland, the sense of touch, and the air element. Physically speaking, it supports our heart, lungs, upper torso, shoulders, hands, and arms. This chakra is also the energetic center of your subtle body, where it serves as perhaps the most powerful link between the physical and spiritual realms.

When the heart chakra is balanced, love flows, and so does the ability to express joy. Self-acceptance, empathy, and sympathy are enhanced.

Balance Your Heart Chakra

There are many ways to balance the heart chakra, which is comprised of the air element. Heart chakra healing brings an abundance of empathy, compassion, and love. Empower your heart chakra with a gratitude practice. Stir feelings of appreciation by keeping a daily gratitude journal about the people, places, and circumstances that you are grateful for. Heart-opening yoga poses like backbends open the energy and space around the heart chakra. Heart chakra meditations, loving self-affirmations, and visualizations of joy and gratitude nourish the heart chakra.

Essential Tips

1. The heart chakra aligns with vibrant emerald green, which represents transformation and love energy. As the bridge between the upper and lower chakras, the heart chakra's color is derived from a combination of the solar plexuses yellow fire element directly below it and the blue of the throat chakra just above it.
2. The heart chakra resonates with the F note at a frequency of 639 Hz, activating healing and love.
3. Chanting or humming the seed mantra YAM creates a harmonic resonance that heals the physical and spiritual heart center.
4. The affirmation for the heart chakra is "I am loving."
5. The heart chakra thrives on raw green foods. Organic greens can help greatly with energy and stress and provide our bodies with whole, balanced nutrients. Drink plenty of fresh, green juice, make a salad, or start your day with a green smoothie. Foods with exceptional ability to heal and balance the heart chakra include kale, broccoli, spinach, chard, parsley, celery, cucumber, zucchini, matcha, green tea, avocado, lime, mint, peas, kiwi, spirulina, and green apples. Green tea, basil, thyme, and cilantro are also nourishing for the heart chakra.
6. Asanas for strengthening the fourth chakra include camel pose, cobra pose, wheel, and upward-facing dog pose.

7. Essential oils known to balance the heart chakra include rosemary and rose. The crystals green aventurine, amazonite (also known as amazonstone), rose quartz, rhodonite, jade, and green calcite do the same.

Chanting OM Meditation

You may recall that the mantra OM is considered the primordial sound of the universe. It represents the essence of all creation and the interconnectedness of existence. Chanting OM creates a healing vibration that nourishes every single cell in the body and affects others. It is the basis for powerful healing meditation.

Take a deep breath in. On the exhale, make sure that the sound you make begins in the pit of your abdomen and moves up through your chest and throat and into your head. In three parts, slowly sing, chant, or hum the word "AUM" or "OM."

Begin with your mouth wide open and sing, chant, or hum the sound "Aah." Feel the sound as it vibrates in your stomach area.

As the sound moves up, around your mouth to sing, chant, or hum the sound "Ou." Feel the sound vibrating into your chest area and then into your throat.

Now allow your mouth to close as you sing, chant, or hum an elongated "Mmm." Feel the sound vibrating in your head and face.

Continue singing, chanting, or humming this AUM or OM to create a vibration you can feel.

Throat Chakra: Expression

nam·as·te: the light in me honors the light in you

The fifth chakra, or the throat chakra, is known in Sanskrit as the *Vishuddha* chakra, which means pure. Associated with the element of ether or space, it represents expansiveness, communication, and the vibration of sound. You'll find the throat chakra at the base of the neck. Physically, it connects with the body's sense of hearing and the thyroid gland. A balanced throat chakra allows you to speak your truth—what is purely you—with grace and ease. As such, the *Vishuddha* chakra is the subtle body's communication center.

Working with the fifth chakra develops creative abilities and enhances deep communication and self-expression.

Balance Your Throat Chakra

Learning how to open, tone, and balance the throat chakra is crucial for the healthy functioning of the mind, body, and spirit. The fifth energy center is especially important as communication impacts all aspects of life.

Repeating positive affirmations is a beneficial healing modality for any chakra, but it is particularly potent for the throat chakra since it governs sound and resonance, and affirmations are repeated aloud. Neck stretches, practicing deep breathing, singing, and including the color blue in your life soothe and tone the throat chakra.

Essential Tips

1. Think, feel, imagine, or visualize the throat chakra as bright blue like the sky. Blue symbolizes serenity and calmness, akin to the soothing qualities of oceans and lakes.
2. The throat chakra resonates with the G note, which vibrates around 741 Hz. This frequency promotes speaking the truth and empowerment.
3. Chanting HAM, the seed mantra for the throat chakra, is thought to awaken intuition and cleanse the fifth chakra.
4. The affirmation associated with the throat chakra is "I speak my truth always."
5. Blue foods heal and nourish the throat energy point. Blueberries, blackberries, plums, fruit smoothies, herbal teas with honey and/or lemons, cantaloupe, watermelon, honeydew, pears, apples, and apricots, as well as tart fruits such as peaches, lemons, kiwi, grapefruit, and limes, are very nourishing for the throat chakra.
6. Inversion poses strengthen the throat chakra as they release tension and bring energy to the thyroid area. These poses include shoulder stand, upward lotus pose, plow pose, fish pose, bridge pose, cobra pose, and reclining angle pose.
7. Try healing the throat chakra with essential oils of peppermint, eucalyptus, and spearmint or crystals such as lapis lazuli, aquamarine, amazonite, and sodalite.

Loving-Kindness Meditation

Carve out some quiet time for yourself. Even a few minutes will work. Close your eyes, relax your muscles, and take a few deep breaths.

Imagine yourself experiencing complete physical and emotional wellness and inner peace. Imagine feeling perfect love for yourself, thanking yourself for all that you are, and knowing that you are just right, just as you are. Focus on this feeling of inner peace and imagine that you are breathing in feelings of love and breathing out any tension or stress in your body and mind.

Repeat three or four positive, reassuring phrases to yourself. Here are a few examples—feel free to create your own:

May I be happy

May I be safe

May I be healthy, peaceful, and strong

May I give and receive appreciation today

May you be well, may you be happy

May you be free from suffering

May you be free of pain and sorrow

May you be peaceful and at ease

May you feel loved

May you be surrounded by loving-kindness

May you feel safe and cared for

May you find true happiness

Next, bask in feelings of warmth and self-compassion for a few moments. If your attention drifts, gently redirect it back to these feelings of loving-kindness and let them completely envelop you.

You can either stay with this focus for the duration of your meditation or shift your focus to your loved ones. Begin with someone who you are very close to, such as a child, spouse, parent, or best friend. Feel your gratitude and love for them. Stay with that feeling. You may want to repeat the reassuring phrases.

Once you have held these feelings for that person, bring other people important to you into your awareness, one by one, and envision them with perfect wellness and inner peace. Then branch out to other friends, family members, neighbors, and acquaintances. If you're inspired to do so, include groups of people from around the world. Extend feelings of loving-kindness to them and focus on feelings of interconnectedness and compassion.

You may even want to include people with whom you are in conflict to help reach a place of forgiveness or greater peace.

When you feel that your meditation is complete, open your eyes. Remember, you can revisit the wonderful feelings you generated at any time. Internalize how loving-kindness meditation *feels* and return to those feelings by shifting your focus and taking a few deep breaths.

Third Eye Chakra: Intuition

an·an·da: bliss

The sixth chakra is called *Ajna* in Sanskrit. Associated with the third eye and the element of light, *Ajna* is located mid-forehead, between the eyebrows, where it represents intuition. In fact, Ajna means "perception or beyond wisdom or insight." If you've ever experienced a "sixth sense," you've come into direct contact with the Ajna chakra, which allows clear thought, inner vision, spiritual guidance, and wisdom. Some call this extrasensory perception or ESP.

The third eye chakra has a feminine energy. When properly balanced, the *Ajna* chakra opens one to clear thought, inner vision, spiritual guidance, wisdom, insight, and access to pure consciousness.

Physically, the sixth chakra is associated with the brain, nervous system, and pituitary gland, which is considered the master regulating gland because it secretes a hormone that monitors the activities of the body's other glands. As the command center of the subtle body, it governs our brains, balancing rational and logical thought with intuitive non-linear thought, sometimes known as the left and right brain, and enhancing deep communication. It also encompasses the eyes and head.

Ajna is also related to our ability to focus on and see the bigger picture. Once you can open the third eye chakra, it becomes easier to connect with the present moment instead of living in the past or present.

Balance Your Third Eye Chakra

Consistent meditation and yoga practice are excellent ways to balance the sixth chakra. Mindfulness—doing one thing at a time with your full attention in the present moment—balances and calms the sixth chakra. The third eye chakra is where our often-busy monkey minds reside, so any practices that calm our nervous systems, such as getting adequate daylight and sleep or practicing alternate nostril breathing (Pranayama), are helpful.

Essential Tips

1. The third eye chakra is represented by vibrant indigo blue. Indigo is the color of the deep midnight sky, of intuition and perception, and it is said to be helpful in opening the third eye chakra. Visualizing that blue light flowing in and out of the center of the forehead cleanses the third eye chakra of stuck energy.
2. The third eye chakra resonates with the A note, which has a peaceful and calming resonance. With a natural resonant frequency of 852 Hz, it triggers a higher realm of spiritual thinking.
3. The seed mantra supporting the third eye chakra is SHAM, the mantra of peace, detachment, and liberation. It's pronounced "'"shum." It calms the mind and promotes mental stability.
4. The affirmation for the third eye chakra is "I see clearly."
5. Foods that support and heal the sixth chakra include nuts, seeds, legumes, and metal detoxers from the ground, such as mushrooms or harvest grains. And, of course, purple-colored fruits like goji berries, acai, blackberries, figs, plums, and Concord grapes nourish the third eye chakra. So do eggplants, purple kale, cabbage, purple potatoes, lavender-infused teas, and brain-boosting antioxidants like dark chocolate. Herbs and spices known to strengthen this chakra include mugwort, poppy seeds, juniper, rosemary, and lavender.
6. Asanas that strengthen the third eye chakra include plow pose, child's pose, downward dog, bow pose, dolphin pose,

sun salutations, and standing head to knee pose.

7. Essential oils thought to balance and heal the third eye chakra include lavender, clary sage, frankincense, juniper, cypress, and cedarwood. Crystals of lapis lazuli and amethyst are also helpful.

Mindful Journaling Exercise

For this loving-kindness mindfulness exercise, locate an inviting journal or notebook and one of your favorite pens. Set a timer for ten minutes. Take a deep breath, close your eyes, and bring your attention to your heart center. Envision a vibrant indigo color enlivening your entire brow area. Then use the following writing prompts to begin the writing process. If an answer comes to you, write it down. If no answer comes, simply move on to the next question with ease.

Who and what am I most grateful for in my life?

How am I best able to express my feelings from the heart?

How can I best serve and care for myself and others?

What is the highest form of self-care that I can offer myself on this day?

What is the highest expression of love that I can offer to others on this day?

What do I really want?

Crown Chakra: Wisdom

praj·na: wisdom

The seventh chakra is called *Sahasrara* in Sanskrit, which translates to "thousand petaled" in English. Located just above the top of the head, it is also known as the crown chakra or pure consciousness. Physically, it represents the pineal gland and a sense of union. This is where many believe the divine or Christ/God or Sacred consciousness enters the human body, and it is thus associated with the element of cosmic energy or thought. When the seventh chakra is balanced, one experiences deep wisdom and knowledge. The energy of the crown chakra is thought to be more masculine in nature.

Balance Your Crown Chakra

There are many ways to balance the crown chakra. A regular meditation practice, preferably once in the morning and once in the afternoon, for at least twenty minutes, works well. Connecting with nature and using aromatherapy helps balance and soothe the crown chakra. Long, slow, deep breathing nourishes the crown chakra. Moving the body through cardiovascular exercises, such as jumping, moves the energy that can get stuck in the crown chakra.

Essential Tips

1. Think, feel, imagine, or visualize the crown chakra as a deep, vibrant purple, sparkling and iridescent. Purple is often associated with royalty and spiritual enlightenment.

In color psychology, purple stimulates the imagination, promotes spiritual awareness, and enhances creativity.

2. The seventh chakra resonates with the B note. Its frequency of 963 Hz is associated with activating the pineal gland, raising consciousness, and awakening intuition.
3. The seed mantra for the crown chakra is the universal sound of OM or AUM.
4. The affirmation associated with the crown chakra is "I am."
5. The best way to open the crown chakra is to consider fasting or intermittent fasting. The seventh chakra thrives on high-alkaline and structured water, high-alkaline foods like leafy greens, and high-chromium foods like broccoli, potatoes, and garlic.
6. The yoga poses known to strengthen the crown chakra include inversions like headstand and other poses like baby eagle, warrior one with eagle arms, and saddle pose.
7. Essential oils known to heal and balance the crown chakra include frankincense, ylang-ylang, lavender, sandalwood, rosemary, lemon, chamomile, myrrh, rosewood, basil, ginger root, patchouli, cedarwood, clary sage, peppermint, rose oil, and jasmine. Look to clear quartz, moonstone, amethyst, selenite, moonstone, agate, lepidolite, howlite, labradorite, sugilite, white agate, fluorite, lapis lazuli, charoite, white calcite, and clear quartz for support from crystals.

A Chakra Toning Exercise

I learned this exercise at the Chopra Center for Wellbeing in Carlsbad, California. The chanted mantras in the following exercise correspond with each chakra in the body. Please see the color chart below that corresponds to each color in the chakra system.

You can find an audio version of this exercise on my website at www.theyogaofmarketing.com/bonuses.

Sit with your eyes closed, cross-legged, or however you feel comfortable and breathe deeply, in through your nose and out through your nose. Sit up straight, put your shoulders back and down, and gently pull in your stomach. Imagine a golden thread reaching from the top of your head to the sky or heavens. Place your tongue gently on the little ridge at the tip of your mouth just behind the two front teeth.

Now, focus on the root, or Muladhara chakra, located at the base of the spine. Envision vibrant red. Chant the mantra LAM as loudly as you can while still feeling comfortable and unself-conscious. Toning the first chakra increases stability, which then leads to flexibility, coherence, and balance in the mind and body.

Now, take another deep breath in, and we'll move up to the second chakra, the *Svadhisthana,* or sacral chakra, located in the lower abdomen. While keeping your eyes closed and breathing deeply, think, feel, imagine, or visualize the vibrant color orange. Chant, hum, or sing the mantra VAM. Toning this chakra will purify the nervous system and nourish every single cell in the body.

With your eyes still closed, take another deep breath in. Move up to your upper abdomen, where the third chakra, the Manipura or solar plexus chakra in Sanskrit, is located. Visualize vibrant yellow. With your focus on your power or third chakra, chant, sing, or hum the mantra RAM. Strengthening the third chakra helps with setting intentions and fulfilling desires.

Now, let's take another deep breath in and flow up to the heart area where the fourth chakra lies. Here, in the heart's center, also known as the *Anahata* chakra, visualize vibrant green. Sing, chant, or hum the mantra YAM. Awakening your heart chakra will increase your experience of peace, harmony, laughter, and love.

While keeping your eyes softly closed and continuing to breathe deeply, move up to your throat or Vishuddha chakra. Imagine vibrant blue in this area. Sing, hum, or chant the mantra HAM using a natural, comfortable tone for your voice. Enlivening the fifth chakra will invigorate creativity, affluence, abundance, and discernment.

Now, we'll flow up to the third eye, or *Anja* chakra, located just above and between the eyebrows. Visualize a beautiful indigo blue in this area. Sing, hum, or chant the mantra SHAM. SHAM is the mantra for peace, detachment, and liberation. Purifying and clearing out your sixth chakra integrates the qualities of truth, unboundedness, and knowingness in your life.

Continuing to breathe deeply while keeping your eyes closed, make your way up to the crown or *Sahasrara* chakra, located just above the head. Now, imagine a truly gorgeous royal purple or violet color with an iridescent glow radiating from this area. Chant, sing, or hum, the mantra OM. Toning the *Sahasrara* chakra enlivens wisdom. Some medical practitioners trained in Ayurveda, a natural system of medicine that originated in India more than 3,000 years ago, believe that balancing this chakra allows us to experience enlightenment and a connection to infinity, immortality, and holiness.

Notice how you feel after this chakra toning exercise. My students report feeling lighter, more focused, and more centered than they did before the exercise. I've learned that attaining higher states of vibration through chakra toning can have many benefits, including strengthening the immune system.

Chakras Are Universal

After studying the chakras for many years, I was fascinated to learn recently that chakra energy not only shows up in and around our human bodies but also manifests in mystical ways all around the globe. Each of the seven major chakras corresponds with a different continent and qualities that reflect the conditions of the chakras in our bodies.

Why is this significant? Recognizing patterns visible throughout creation helps us see the vast and interconnected nature of the universe. We are part of something much larger than ourselves.

The locations listed in the chart below are said to exude a level of vibrational energy aligning with the qualities of each chakra. Interestingly enough, these sites have long been considered sacred. They're linked to spiritual awakening, healing, and transformation.

Chakra	Geographic Placement	Possible Reasons Why
1. Root	Mount Shasta, California	Location is intrinsic to Native American traditions and beliefs about grounding, survival, and stability.
2. Sacral	Lake Titicaca, Peru and Bolivia	Ancient Incan civilizations associated this location with myths about fertility and creation.
3. Solar Plexus	Uluru and Kata Tjuta, Australia	Anangu people believe Uluru is a sacred source of spiritual strength and energy, fueling personal power and self-worth.

Chakra	Geographic Placement	Possible Reasons Why
4. Heart	Glastonbury and Shaftesbury, England	Glastonbury is linked to Avalon in Arthurian legends. With Shaftesbury, it is considered a spiritual center of divine love where earthly and spiritual energies are balanced.
5. Throat	Great Pyramid of Giza, Egypt, Mt. Sinai, and the Mount of Olives in Jerusalem	Sites of ancient wisdom, prophecy, and divine messages.
6. Third Eye	Combined border of Iran, Afghanistan, and Pakistan	Area has a rich history of mystical traditions from Zoroastrianism and Sufism to Vedic. Considered a gateway to enlightenment.
7. Crown	Mount Kailash, Tibet	Considered a center of spiritual power and cosmic energy in Hinduism, Buddhism, Jainism, and Bon traditions.

While not scientifically proven, some spiritual seekers believe that visiting or meditating at these locations has the potential to expand healing, personal transformation, and collective consciousness.

Marketing Disciplines

Does the word "marketing" conjure negative thoughts?

It doesn't have to, and that's the whole purpose of The Yoga of Marketing.

Over the years, I've worked with many clients who would much rather stick to writing their books or focusing on improving their products and services than think about marketing. These days, most people seem convinced they must build huge followings on social media to succeed. They feel let down or even inadequate when people don't "like" or comment on their posts.

But here's the thing: marketing is more about developing and nurturing long-term, reciprocal, and meaningful relationships than it is about sales. If you connect with people deeply and show them you care, sales will naturally follow—for their benefit and yours. And for most people, focusing on relationships is far less intimidating than thinking about sales and marketing.

So, stand back and look at marketing from a different perspective. Instead of posting content to sell or even just to remain visible online, focus on getting to know your clients and customers. Start conversations with them virtually through their websites or social media posts. Engage with them offline. Call them up to see how they're doing. Send a note or card by mail—the old-fashioned kind, not email. The conversation shouldn't always revolve around you or your offerings.

Take the sting out of content creation with thoughtful strategic planning. Create a simple blog or podcast and keep an editorial calendar with topics and a schedule for content creation. Post regularly and draw information from your relevant content to create shorter posts for whatever social media channels you feel most comfortable using. And remember, it isn't just about you. Interact with others in your field. Respond to your clients and customers online. Create tribes and communities of people interested in your topics and communicate with them via digital newsletters or select from a variety of online forums, ranging from Facebook, Signal, or WhatsApp groups to platforms such as Discord or Slack.

With regular and meaningful engagement, your specific audience will come to recognize who you are and what differentiates you from others offering similar products and services. They'll learn to trust you, and sales will result organically.

Now, let's take a look at the seven marketing (relationship-building) centers—each of which aligns with a chakra center.

3

Marketing Centers

Just as there are seven chakras or energy centers to align body, mind, and spirit, the following seven marketing centers align the promotional strategies for your business in a way that also keeps *you* in alignment and reduces the stress involved with undertaking something you may not be naturally comfortable with.

The Foundation

"It's time to start living the life you've imagined." – Henry James

Just as you must build a strong foundation in your energy body and the root chakra, you must create a strong foundation for your marketing efforts. Of course, by the time you begin focusing on marketing, you will have implemented any fundamental legal requirements for establishing your business.[5] You'll also

5 See the US Small Business Administration website for more information: https://www.sba.gov/.

have a mission statement in place to define your purpose and core goals, what you do, and who you serve; and a vision statement to describe your long-term objectives and how you want your business to look in the future.

A foundation for marketing is structured upon a research plan and a database of potential customers related to your mission and vision and analyzing their needs. Doing so will help you find ways to meet those needs and establish the relationships that are critical to developing your business and serving others.

Over the years, I've discovered that the expression, "Your network is your net worth," is true. Developing a strong network of contacts creates a nearly built-in target audience for your messages, products, and services that will serve you well for the life of your business.

Case Study: Soul-Centered

In the fall of 2011, my friend, meditation instructor, and then client, Sarah McLean, bestselling author and founder of the McLean Meditation Institute, hired me to assist her and her publisher, Hay House, with the launch and release of her first book, *Soul-Centered: Transform Your Life in 8 Weeks with Meditation.*

Sarah had already established a very strong professional network and database of meditation and mindfulness professionals. Her platform was expansive and solid. She had worked closely with experts and influencers in the personal growth and development, self-discovery, and spirituality arenas, including Deepak Chopra, Debbie Ford, Gary Zukav, and Byron Katie.

Because Sarah already had a well-established database, we could focus on her strategic marketing plan. We implemented a "spike day" campaign to increase rankings and visibility on

Amazon and created a national public relations and media campaign. Her campaign focused not only on media outlets in Sarah's area of expertise but also on major national outlets to create name recognition and brand awareness for Sarah and her book. We intended to brand her as the face of mainstream meditation.

Our targeted marketing and communications efforts worked. We landed media placements and coverage for Sarah in *The Arizona Republic, Costco Connection Magazine, The New York Times*, ABC-15, Dallas Morning News, *Prevention Magazine*, BeliefNet, *OM Times Magazine*, *Huffington Post* (US and UK), *Reader's Digest, Santa Barbara Magazine*, the *San Francisco Chronicle, LA Times, Better Connecticut, MORE Magazine, Unity Magazine, Montecito Journal, Daily OM, Organic Spa Magazine, Sonoran Living*, and other national and international media outlets. Her publisher also offered her the opportunity to publish her next book, *The Power of Attention*, which she did.

Create a Database

Whether you're marketing books, coaching services, or widgets, you can achieve the same kind of success Sarah did—even if you don't have an existing platform—by creating a database.

A database is a collection of well-organized information about clients and potential clients that can be accessed and sorted by computer or an online platform. Clients or customers make up the lifeblood of any business. Solid information and research about them form the root of all growth plans.

Full-featured customer relationship management databases store and process customer contact details, and—depending on the type of software or interface used—they can also track interaction history with existing clients, new prospects or leads, business opportunities, and even personal details about who they are as individuals. Some customer relationship management databases can also run and track marketing (relationship-building) campaigns.

The database helps you learn about your clients and customers, including who they are, why they purchase your products, and where you can engage with them online or in person. This allows businesses to build relationships, better anticipate customer needs, and, as a result, fulfill them.

Although the idea of building a database may feel overwhelming, it doesn't have to be if you begin with who you know.

When I began a real estate career in Phoenix, Arizona in the mid-nineties, my mentor referred to a database as a *sphere of influence.* Essentially, a sphere of influence is a list of people we know. That includes co-workers, peers, industry associates, followers, customers, vendors, influencers and connections.

The people within our spheres, especially those with whom our opinion generally holds weight or significance, have the power to affect our businesses in positive ways. So, identify your sphere and enter your connections into a database. Then you can begin to engage with key people more meaningfully and consistently to expand your database.

Maintaining a healthy sphere of influence is about caring for and nurturing your relationships. As that happens, people learn more about your products or services, use them, and send others your way. Referrals are key to natural, organic growth. If your current sphere of influence has one hundred people, and each of those people knows another hundred people, you have ten thousand opportunities for referrals.

Today, the words "list" and "platform" tend to be used synonymously with the database or sphere of influence. The old saying,

"It's not *what* you know, it's *who* you know," is certainly true, and it's pertinent to the marketing process. In today's social media environment, followers have become increasingly important to the marketing process. Creating an online community or tribe of like-minded people is an important marketing strategy and a way to expand your database. That strategy can be quite successful, although it can take three to five years to fully develop.

Additionally, the term *influence* carries over to *influencers*, individuals who have weight or influence on social media channels such as LinkedIn, Facebook (now officially known as Meta), Twitter (now officially known as X), and Instagram.

So, gather all your contacts and everything you know about them in one place. This can be as simple as using an Excel spreadsheet, an online newsletter database, or perhaps a more sophisticated online database capable of tracking myriad information. There are hundreds, maybe thousands, of different options available for storing contact data.

It's imperative to the marketing process that all your team members support your database with impeccable notes and information on an ongoing basis. These contacts become a built-in, nearly guaranteed target market for products and services. Your database can help you organize, categorize, and prioritize contacts while nurturing and monitoring relationships with previous, current, and prospective customers and clients.

Conduct Research

Once your client database is in place, conduct research to determine similar characteristics among them. Doing so identifies your target market and makes it easier to create strategic business and marketing plans. The data tells you what your customers need and want, thus defining marketing opportunities. It helps create and evaluate marketing actions. Depending on how well various marketing strategies perform, it becomes possible to forecast trends and develop a strong marketing plan with clear goals, strategies, and tactics.

Entire books have been written about how to find, record, and analyze data for marketing products and services. Depending upon your timeline and budget, you can hire professionals to conduct marketing research and identify your ideal customer by analyzing your existing clients' characteristics and behaviors. But if you don't have the budget, don't worry. Books are available on Amazon and in bookstores about how to find, record, and analyze marketing data. And a few basic steps will get you started.

Step One: Define Your Market

Use your existing customer data to determine demographics, psychographics (likes and dislikes), challenges, and current buying habits. Study demographics using data available from your website, data management system, and email subscribers.

Step Two: Determine Why Customers Like Your Product or Service

The next step is to determine what makes your customers choose you over other brands so you can keep giving them what they want and learn what other products or services they might wish for. Speak with them directly or conduct surveys to determine how they use your products, their favorite features, and anything else you might like to know. They might value your unique pricing model, cost savings, greater satisfaction, or social benefits, such as sustainability or improved productivity. These factors are your *value propositions*.

Study demographics through data available in Google Analytics, customer data in your Customer Relationship Management or CRM Platform, your existing email subscribers, the different ways customers use your products, and which features they use, along with any other information you can find about your buyers and consumers.

Step Three: Determine Wants and Needs

Abraham Maslow, a specialist in human behavioral psychology, developed a Hierarchy of Needs in 1943 that may help you understand what your customers want and need—and why.

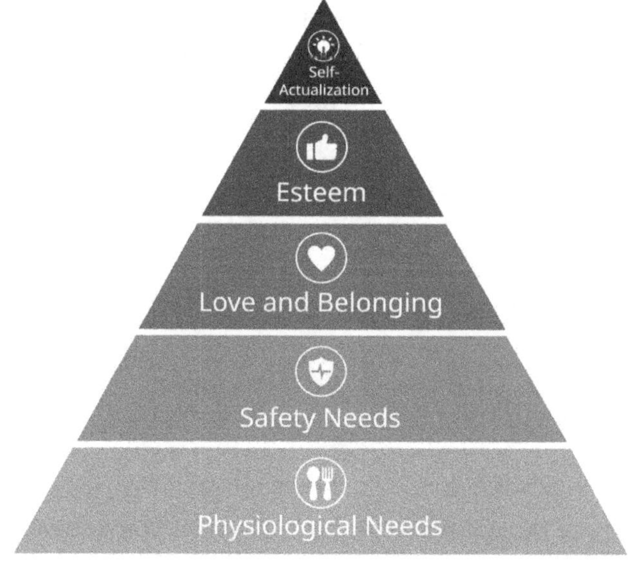

According to Maslow, each human being has different motivations, as illustrated in the pyramid. As with chakras, it's important to establish the foundation before moving to the next level. As illustrated in Maslow's pyramid, the foundation requires meeting basic physiological needs for survival. Only when those needs are met can one's attention shift to acquiring basic safety.

When one is safe, they have room to pursue social interaction, followed by self-esteem, and finally, self-actualization—the realization or fulfillment of one's talent and potential. (See how closely those ideas align with chakras?)

Understanding Maslow's hierarchy and where your product and client relationships fall within it can help you identify what motivates your target audience. That information shapes effective marketing strategies like product or service positioning, promotional and advertising campaigns, and realistic pricing strategies. If marketers know the wants and needs of their target market, they can better shape their strategies to meet those wants and needs.

Research provides a clearer understanding of your customers and the people with whom you are building relationships. Knowing who they are, why they come to you, and what they want and need provides the foundational information required to spread the word about your products and services.

Creation

"The desire to create is one of the deepest yearnings of the human soul." – Dieter F. Uchtdorf

The second chakra is all about creation, and that aligns perfectly with the second marketing center where you're creating—or birthing—the shape and character of your marketing strategy. Exploring the Seven Ps of Marketing will help you develop your strategic marketing strategy. Introduced by E. Jerome McCarthy in 1960, a professor of marketing at Michigan State University and the University of Notre Dame, the Seven Ps are terrific tools for developing and evaluating your business activities.

The Seven Ps of Marketing

The Seven Ps of Marketing help us define the marketing mix, including strategies and tactics.

Product

Product represents what you sell, whether it's a product or a service or a combination of both. The product is developed to meet core customer needs. The challenge is to create the right bundle of benefits that meets those needs. What happens as a customer's needs change, competitors get ahead, or new opportunities arise? We must add to the bundle of benefits to improve the offering, create new versions of existing products, or launch brand-new products. When improving the product offering, think beyond the actual product itself. Consider improving its value by differentiating it from competitors' products. That might mean including guarantees, extended warranties, special training, or an app that helps users get the most out of the product.

Price

This is the only revenue-generating element of the mix. All other marketing activities represent a cost. So, it's important to get the price right to not only cover costs but also to generate profit. Before setting prices, research information about what customers are willing to pay and gain an understanding of the demand for that product/service in the marketplace. As price is also a strong indication of the positioning in the market against competitors (low prices=value brands), prices need to be set with competitors in mind as well.

Place

This is the location where your clients and customers make purchases. It could be through a physical store, an app, or a website. Some companies have the physical space or online presence to take product straight to their customers, whereas others must work with intermediaries, such as a distribution company, for delivery. The decisions we need to make in this area include which, if any, intermediaries will be involved in the distribution chain and the logistics involved in getting the products and services to the end customer, including storage and transportation.

Promotion

So we have a fabulous product, an appealing price, available in all the right places, but how do the customers know it exists? Promotion is about communicating messages to customers to generate awareness, interest, desire, or action. We have different tools for communication with varying benefits. Advertising is good for raising awareness and reaching new audiences, whereas personal selling uses a sales team and is great for building relationships with customers and clients and closing a sale. The challenge? To choose the best tools for the job and select the most effective media to reach our audiences based on what we know about them. If your customer is a regular on Instagram, even though you know nothing about social media, it's time you either learn about social media or hire an expert who can help you communicate with your customers on Instagram. (We'll give promotion more attention when we explore the fifth marketing center.)

People

A company's people are at the forefront of customer interaction—taking and processing inquiries, orders, and complaints in person, through online chat, on social media, or via a call center. They interact with customers throughout their journey and become the face of the organization for the customer. Their knowledge of the company's products and services and how to use them, their ability to access relevant information, and their everyday approach and attitude need to be optimized. People can be inconsistent, but with the right training, empowerment, and motivation by a company, they can also represent an opportunity to differentiate an offering in a crowded market and build valuable relationships with customers.

Process

All companies want to create a smooth, efficient, and customer-friendly journey, and this can't be achieved without the right processes behind the scenes to make that happen. Understanding the steps of the customer journey—from making an inquiry online to requesting information and making a purchase—helps us consider what processes need to be in place to ensure that the customer has a positive experience. When a customer makes an inquiry, how long will they have to wait before receiving a response? How long do they wait between booking a meeting with the sales team and the meeting taking place? What happens once they place an order? How do we make sure that reviews are generated after a purchase? How can we use technology to make our processes more efficient? All these considerations help build a positive customer experience.

Physical Evidence

Physical evidence provides tangible clues about the quality of experience that a company is offering. It can be particularly useful when a customer has not bought from the company before and needs some reassurance or is expected to pay for a service before it is delivered. For a restaurant, for example, physical evidence could be in the form of the surroundings, staff uniform, menus, and online reviews to indicate the experience that could be expected. For an agency, the website itself holds valuable physical evidence—from testimonials to case studies, as well as the contracts that companies are given to represent the services they can expect to be delivered.

Case Study: Accomplish Your Heart's Desires

In the spring of 2009, I got a call from a kind and lovely consultant in Los Angeles, California, asking if I'd work with her to promote and publicize her client's new book release. An editor at Simon & Schuster on Avenue of the Americas in New York City referred the woman to me. I had just finished another Simon & Schuster author's six-month-long book launch and strategic book marketing and public relations campaign, and I welcomed the opportunity for a new creative project. Little did I know that working with this particular author would change the course of my professional career. Working with the author and her team of experts, we garnered national publicity and media opportunities that I had only dreamed of prior to our engagement.

The book is *Heart & Sold* by celebrity real estate expert Valerie Fitzgerald. In the book, Valerie shares her personal journey through emotional and tangible challenges in her life and how she overcame tumultuous situations to regain her personal power.

We implemented a full-blown Amazon Spike Day campaign for the launch of Valerie's new book. As one of Coldwell Banker's Top 100 agents nationwide, we were able to leverage her extensive professional network for success. We secured a radio spot for Valerie on *Oprah Radio* and a print media placement in *Forbes* Magazine. Valerie was recently elected to the Forbes Real Estate Council.

As I have learned through experience, media coverage begets media coverage, like a domino effect. After we secured the initial print and radio media placements, Valerie then appeared on the *HGTV* television hit series *Selling LA* for three seasons, where the show featured her and her team tackling the challenges of selling luxury properties in the highly competitive Los Angeles real estate market.

Valerie has since established her own charity foundation and speaks to thousands of people around the country at numerous business conventions and conferences.

To what can we attribute Valerie's tremendous success in business and life? Through the practice of yoga and the other mindfulness techniques we explored in the first section of this book, Valerie regained her personal power. When that happens, a new kind of self-awareness emerges. As that self-awareness expands, business and life begin to change in positive ways we could never have imagined, just as it did for my client Valerie.

Even if you are not yet a yoga practitioner, the sound marketing principles in the book are easy to implement for success.

One of the endorsements Valerie received for her book, from Vanna White, encapsulates the connection between *The Yoga of Marketing* process and Valerie's success: "After reading this book, you will feel that you too can accomplish anything that your heart desires."

Through *The Yoga of Marketing* process, we begin to focus on what is already working in your business and how to accomplish anything you'd like in business and in life. Once you begin to focus on connecting the mind, body, and spirit, successes and victories begin to emerge in all aspects of life. When you implement the mindful approaches in this book, your full creative potential will be unleashed.

Power

"Change the world by being yourself." —Amy Poehler

In the chakra system, the third center is associated with one's sense of personal power, self-esteem, and reliability. To maximize your power as a marketer and develop a good marketing strategy, you must be intimately aware of these qualities in yourself and your business. You must understand your strengths and weaknesses and determine the most appropriate place to focus your efforts.

Case Study: Perfect Positioning

I helped The Sextant Group (now an NV5 company) develop a marketing and public relations campaign to do just that. Originally, The Sextant Group offered a broad range of technological, professional, and technical engineering consulting services. Through ongoing strategic marketing planning, analysis, and refinement of its marketing plans through the years, the company was able to shine a light on its core competencies: audiovisual consulting, information technologies, security, acoustical consulting, and specialty lighting consulting. Although their team of experts was well-versed in many other specialties, such as telemedicine, studio design, and performing arts spaces, their commitment to their core competencies differentiated them from competitors in the architectural, engineering, and construction (AEC) industry.

Using a series of thought leadership strategies and tactics, such as keynote speaking, thought leadership articles in key industry and trade publications as well as leadership roles in industry-specific organizations, this company was able to continuously exceed their sales goals and was eventually purchased by a large global engineering firm, NV5, who provides solutions for public and private sector clients who support infrastructure, utility, and building assets and systems on a massive scale.

Through a targeted national marketing and public relations campaign, we were able to secure media placements for The Sextant Group in *Architizer, ArchDaily, Commercial Integrator Magazine, Atlanta Business Journal, BDC Network, AVNetwork, Los Angeles Business Journal, Pittsburgh Post-Gazette, Pittsburgh Business Times, Phoenix Business Journal, AIA KnowledgeNet, Lighting and Sound America, Quattro Quarterly Magazine (front cover placement), University Business Magazine, Healthcare Design Magazine, Campus Technology Magazine, ESchoolNews, Business News Daily, CoreNet Global Magazine, Washington Business Journal, Sound and Communications Magazine, Automated Buildings Magazine,* and *EC Magazine.*

With careful analysis, you can apply a few different strategies to position your business for success.

Analyze Your Business

You know who your target market is. How well are you meeting their needs? Are there areas where you can improve? What might stand in your way? How can you put your best foot forward to be a strong relationship builder in your field?

These two steps will help you get there.

Step One: Evaluate Your Business's Position

To determine a strategic marketing plan for your business or for a product launch, evaluate your business's position by executing a SWOT or SOAR analysis—ideally, both. A business advisor or consultant can conduct these analyses. If you don't have the budget for a business advisor or consultant to conduct a strategic planning session, pose a series of questions to your team, and together, brainstorm their responses.

A SWOT analysis determines strengths, weaknesses, opportunities, and threats. It's a simple yet powerful tool to help you develop a business strategy that takes advantage of what you already have going for you while expressly looking for threats and weaknesses beyond your control so you can determine how to approach them.

The four simple questions you can ask yourself, your team, and your customers include:

1. What are my internal **strengths**? What do I do best? What are my positive traits?
2. What are my internal **weaknesses**? What tasks do I avoid doing because of a lack of confidence?
3. What are my external **opportunities**? How can I turn my strengths into opportunities?

4. What are my external **threats**? What obstacles do I face that are out of my control?

A SOAR analysis focuses on enhancing what is already being done well by determining your business's strengths, opportunities, aspirations, and results. It utilizes current strengths and future vision to establish strategic goals. It shows you how to leverage current strengths to take advantage of opportunities. As with a SWOT analysis, you'll get the best results from a fresh external perspective as well as team brainstorming sessions.

The four simple questions to ask yourself for a SOAR analysis include:

1. What are our greatest **strengths**?
2. What are our best **opportunities**?
3. What sort of organization do we **aspire** to be?
4. What specific **results** will we see when we get there?

Once you've implemented one or both strategic planning processes, create an action plan to bridge the gap between where your visibility lies now and where you'd like it to be.

Step Two: Determine Your Core Competency

Defining your core competency—your unique capability or advantage—is integral for success. Getting super clear on the core competency is essential. I coach clients to review their mission and vision statements to determine the competence that most strongly influences customer decisions to choose their products and services.

Core competencies are the factors that separate your business from your competitors. These competencies are most often related to a capability or advantage your company has over similar companies in your field or industry. Core competencies are rare, challenging for competitors to imitate, and offer superior value to customers. Most businesses have more than one core competency. However, your company may have a primary core competency that supersedes the rest and is the defining factor that sets it apart.

To find your core competencies, review your mission and vision statements and compare them to the results of your SWOT and SOAR analysis. See where these factors align and identify how they intersect with what your customers like and need. Also identify any areas where improving competency would be advantageous.

Identifying and expanding these competencies is important because it allows you to determine how to allocate your resources in the most beneficial and productive ways. It also enables you to identify the best projects and opportunities to pursue that align with your core competencies.

Spirit

"There are only two mantras, yum and yuck. Mine is yum."
– Tom Robbins

If developing deep, long-lasting relationships is what marketing is all about, spirit is the heart of the fourth marketing center, just as it is with the fourth chakra. This is where you determine what makes you, *you*, and ensure your unique spirit shines through in all you do with effective branding. This branding reflects your "yum." It differentiates you from your competition and proclaims why there is no one else like you.

Also known as a unique selling proposition (USP) or unique value proposition (UVP), your yum is a clear statement that describes the benefit of your offerings, how you solve your customers' needs, and what distinguishes you from the competition. It is a concise, straightforward statement about the benefits you offer customers. What benefits does the customer gain by working with you? A strong yum creates customers' strong desires to purchase your product or service.

In marketing, the yum and yuck principle described by novelist Tom Robbins applies. It should be fairly simple to discern between your *yums* and *yucks.* A strong and distinct yum gives you a unique advantage in the eyes of your target audience and can help elevate you to thought leadership and industry expert status. Being a top expert in your field is a very compelling and powerful competitive advantage. A crystal clear yum will distinguish your brand from all others.

Throughout my career, I have worked with numerous corporations, businesses of all sizes, and clients from every walk of life. Many of my favorite clients are authors—probably because, from a young age, I always enjoyed reading and writing, especially about people and their stories. I like to reflect on the authors who were some of my favorites.

Case Study: Know What Differentiates You

I thoroughly enjoyed working with author Richard Polak, one of the top human resources consultants in the world. We created the national marketing and public relations campaign for his book release launch, *Work Smart Now: How to Jump Start Productivity, Empower Employees, and Achieve More.*

Richard and his book tackle important workplace topics, such as "The Five Buckets of Productivity," "How to Practice Compassion in the Workplace," "Absenteeism versus Presenteeism," "The Consequences of Poor Communication," and "The Importance of Social/Community Wellbeing."

Richard exhibits key qualities that undoubtedly contributed to making my experiences with him so enjoyable. He understands his yums as unique differentiators, as qualities that not only share his work but his spirit, the essence of who he is. Some of them include:

Gratitude. Whether I garnered Richard a small or large article placement in a publication, he was grateful. If I edited an article, he was grateful. No matter what I did for him or his book, Richard's genuine and authentic sense and communication of gratitude were consistent.

Action. Richard understands what I believe is one of the fundamental principles of creating a conscious life: the movement of energy, chi, or prana. Everything is energy and information that is constantly moving and changing. Even marketing is simply the movement of energy. I remember one of my clients, author, psychotherapist, and educator Jude Bijou, who recommended that people simply shake like a dog to change up their energy for a better life. Richard works while walking on a treadmill. He keeps himself moving in body and mind. Oxygen not only feeds the body, but it also feeds brain cells.

Service. Richard understands how to serve others. I remember him asking often what he could do to help me make his book launch campaign better. I never once heard him complain or ask his team to do more. Rather, he constantly offered to be of service to his team and clients.

Mindfulness. Richard implements mindfulness techniques at home and at work. It does not surprise me at all that Richard and his book ended up in *Forbes*, on television in Los Angeles, in *Thrive Global,* Arianna Huffington's online community, the *Associated Press,* and numerous other national publications. This reminds me of the quote by Hermes Trismegistus, "As above, so below, as within, so without, as the universe, so the soul…"

These qualities are all part of Richard's "yum."

Is YOUR yum beginning to come across?

Determine Your Yum

With all the research you've gathered, it's time to determine how well your current messaging and branding align with who you are. Are they helping you build successful relationships? Or do they need some tweaking?

Step One: Assess Your Existing Messaging

Some items to check for include your implicit audiences, value proposition framing, demonstration of value, brand voice, and visual or graphical identity. Some questions you can ask yourself and your team, even customers, include:

Is my message clear and concise?

Does my message communicate my value proposition?

Is my messaging familiar and conversational?

Does my messaging showcase my brand's originality and uniqueness?

Step Two: Create Your Messaging Guide

A messaging guide incorporates your brand's positioning, target audiences, value propositions, key messages, and unique tone of voice. It helps you determine what to say and how to say it to specific segments of your audience, as well as a general audience. The messaging guide acts as a standard for your internal and external communications. You and your team will consult it regularly.

You'll want to communicate the brand's written voice, textual style preference, typography, color palette, and iconography. Here are some key elements to consider when composing a basic messaging guide:

Product Name

Product Tagline

Product Value Proposition

Product Features

Product Benefits

Product FAQs

Step Three: Develop Your Message and Branding

No matter the size of your business, successful branding revolves around a consistent message and identity. Here, we will outline your brand identity, and then you can fill it in with content and other brand assets.

Create a Brand Positioning Statement

A brand statement is your short description or elevator pitch for what you do, how, and why. It should tell what your brand does, who it serves, and the differentiating values and outcomes of those values. By now, you will have developed a clear value proposition, which is both your promise to your audience and your selling point.

Here are some popular brand positioning statements that may sound familiar and spark some ideas:

"At **Nike**, we're committed to creating a better, more sustainable future for our people, planet, and communities through the power of sport."

"For quality beverage seekers, **Coca-Cola** offers a wide range of the most refreshing options. Each creates a great experience for customers when they enjoy a Coca-Cola brand drink. Unlike other beverage options, Coca-Cola products inspire happiness and make a positive difference in customers' lives, and the brand is intensely focused on the needs of consumers and customers."

"**Disney** provides unique entertainment for consumers seeking magical experiences and memories. Disney leads the competition by providing every aspect of related products and services to the world and appealing to people of all ages."

"**McDonald's** is a leader in the fast-food industry, with quick, friendly service and consistency across thousands of convenient locations. McDonald's' dedication to improving operations and customer satisfaction sets it apart from other fast-food restaurants."

Develop Your Brand Elements and a Brand Guide

Develop an easily recognizable brand identity. At every touchpoint, your audience should encounter the same style and message. This coherent brand experience fosters trust. Your audience knows what to expect when they engage with your content. You can look at any brand to find examples of the essential brand elements. Businesses create a variety of signature visual expressions of business identity, including logos, color palettes, fonts, imagery, communication voices, and slogans. After you've established your brand identity, begin to craft quality content. Be strategic. Develop the topics and creative processes that will allow you to scale. Quality content creation can include articles, blog posts, videos, graphics, or social media posts. Write so that all sectors of your audience can understand you.

To create my messaging and branding, I studied my target market demographics. Most of my clients were female, so I chose a brand identity—a creative look and feel—that appealed to women. Since I primarily work with professionals, I selected corporate blue for marketing materials. My time working at American Express taught me that a vibrant blue color resonates strongly with those in professional sectors.

To get my business off the ground, I reached out to people I already knew in the marketplace to determine if they needed assistance with their marketing or public relations efforts. For example, reaching out to one of my former clients put me in contact with the amazing author, public speaker, and spiritual medium, Colette Baron-Reid. You'll hear more about her shortly.

Expression

"The message behind the words is the voice of the heart."– Rumi

The fifth marketing center gathers everything you know about yourself and your business, along with your newly created messaging guide and branding, to determine the most effective way to express your message. Like the relationships foundational to your business, your channels of expression must be maintained and nurtured over the life of the business.

Case Study: Express Yourself!

Colette Baron-Reid is one of the most creative people I have ever met. She has appeared on global stages, television screens, radio channels, and in films. She was even an EMI Records Ltd. recording artist. She frequently communicates with people who have passed and starred in an entire television series about communicating with spirits. She is a true, modern-day mystic who writes music, meditates, paints, and researches the Unified Field Theory. To me, she is a goddess.

In 2013, Colette asked me to assist with the marketing and public relations campaign for her new book, *Weight Loss for People Who Feel Too Much.*[6] I was honored and delighted. At the time, Colette was one of the most respected intuition experts and renowned psychics in the world. Besides being a beautiful human being inside and out, Colette could accurately read a person's entire life purpose and understand their challenges in less than a minute.

---

6 Colette Baron-Reid, *Weight Loss for People Who Feel Too Much: A 4-Step, 8-Week Plan to Finally Lose the Weight, Manage Emotional Eating, and Find Your Fabulous Self* (New York: Harmony, 2013).

As part of a national public relations and media campaign for Colette's new book, we generated a series of press releases that would emphasize her expertise not only in the metaphysical plane but also as a renowned author, energy expert, and keynote speaker. This is one example of integrating key messaging and branding into a campaign.

Our targeted communications and public relations strategy worked. *The TODAY Show* and numerous other national media outlets featured Colette and her book, *Weight Loss for People Who Feel Too Much.*

Knowing who you are and the gifts apparent in your products and services will help you shape unique messaging and branding for yourself and/or your clients.

Communication Channels

Above and beyond standard client communications, such as newsletters, holiday cards, and email communications, there are three primary ways to communicate with your database of clients and customers: advertising, sales promotions, and public relations.

Advertising

This is one of the most prominent and widely used communication tools in a marketing campaign. It can come in both paid and unpaid forms. The main driving force behind this tool is mass media, such as television, radio, digital, and print media campaigns. Advertising is a marketing practice that employs various techniques and messages to get the public's attention and persuade them to respond to products, services, opinions, or causes in a certain way.

Sales Promotions

Sales promotions are direct communication tools and marketing strategies utilizing certain incentives to encourage customers to buy a service or product. These tools are used to communicate with the consumer directly and effectively to promote a product or service. Some techniques may include temporary discounts, telemarketing, gift vouchers or coupons, distributing free samples, early-bird specials, and buy-one-get-one-free promotions.

Public Relations

This kind of marketing campaign includes a whole host of strategies to accomplish an organization's goals by sending messages and press releases to appropriate audiences, including the media. Public relations (PR) professionally represents and handles a company's positive public image. It is an important element of the promotional mix that helps a business maintain good relationships with the public and the media. This includes garnering editorial placements in newspaper articles, television segments, radio spots, and internet media exposure such as blogs, e-magazines, and podcasts.

PR focuses on building and maintaining positive relationships with stakeholders and the broader community, which can lead to sustained goodwill and a positive reputation over time. Because PR involves third-party endorsements, such as media coverage or influencer recommendations, it builds credibility. Readers, viewers, and consumers perceive this kind of exposure to be more credible than paid advertisements.

If you don't have a budget for advertising, PR strategies can be more cost-effective than advertising, too—although PR takes a lot of time to generate desired outcomes.

❊

Knowing the three avenues you can use to express your message, let's take a look at the different strategies available for each. As you'll see, some overlap occurs between them.

Advertising

These days, technological advances have made a wide array of marketing possibilities available to even the smallest of businesses. Before you determine *how* you want to communicate with your clientele, take a look at the options you have to choose from—and notice how many of them utilize online technologies.

Amazon Optimization

Amazon is the largest online retailer in the world, with a catalog that includes more than thirty-three million book titles and more than 350 million other products. Optimizing your Amazon presence as much as possible can help increase your product position in Amazon search results and, therefore, overall visibility on the site.

To start, research and select targeted keywords and the most relevant browsing categories for your product or your book title. Use these keywords in your product or book description so that buyers can easily find it within the appropriate market sector (or genre if you're marketing a book) and increase the accuracy of search results. Be sure to build out your Amazon page thoroughly too. Include biographical information, photos, videos, event updates, and a blog feed linked to your website if available.

I also recommend Amazon sellers and authors secure one hundred positive Amazon reviews. This number positively impacts Amazon's algorithms and helps drive more traffic to whatever you are selling. In addition, ensure your Amazon Detail Page is accurate, complete, and includes all your key search terms. This page educates consumers about your product, book, or brand with enhanced graphics and copy, thus differentiating your goods from competitors in the market, improving search engine optimization (SEO), and increasing visibility.

Amazon Targeted Ads

Amazon's targeted advertising allows sellers to reach customers and readers who are ready to buy. Based on keyword searches and complementary products, including bestsellers in your book or product genre, you can display your wares to Amazon users in various places throughout their Amazon browsing experience. This drives sales and increases your visibility on Amazon.

Amazon offers a wide array of advertising options from paying for product sponsorship and higher visibility to creating an Amazon store on the Amazon website and creating custom advertising. Amazon advertising options include sponsored products, sponsored brands, sponsored displays, stores, audio ads, video ads, custom advertising, Amazon DSP (demand-side platform), and Amazon Attribution.

Other Targeted Ads

Depending on how much time is available before the product launch or book release date and how much budget is allocated for online advertising, I usually recommend Amazon, Google, and LinkedIn ad campaigns that will build brand awareness, target prospective buyers, and link potential buyers directly to your retail product or book pages. If you happen to have an e-book, your customers can instantly purchase and download it.

Sales Promotion

Creating and implementing promotional packages and activities generate online energy for your product or book. There are numerous tactics that will work. Here are a few that my clients have found to be effective.

Price Promotion

Your distributors or publisher will likely provide opportunities to offer a limited-time price promotion with major retailers like Amazon, iBookstore, and Barnes & Noble.

Giveaways

Depending on their budget, many clients will create free giveaways to create buzz around their product launches and book releases and to build their email lists. Clients sometimes partner with major sponsors to underwrite their giveaways. One of my clients gave away a cruise as part of his product launch campaign. Another client raffled off a pair of Nike tennis shoes as part of her virtual book launch party. Get creative!

Online Excerpt and Product Positioning Posting

Online excerpts are extremely important for increasing your product or book's discoverability and visibility in search results from online sellers and major search engines. Excerpts allow potential buyers the opportunity to preview short samples of your book or product's content and to make their buying decisions. Excerpts also allow for the content of your product or book to be indexed online. It's important to list your excerpts on Amazon, Barnes & Noble, Goodreads, and Google, as well as with independent booksellers, wholesalers, and distributors like Ingram,

Baker and Taylor, National Book Network, Gardners, OverDrive, and Bookazine.

Public Relations

I recommend Source of Sources (SOS), a free PR tool that has helped me garner national and international media placements for my clients.[7] Developed by Peter Shankman, this tool offers daily media queries from journalists looking for expert sources for their stories. It connects businesses, experts, journalists, and publicists.

There are several other ways to implement PR strategies and tactics.

Journalists

Connecting with writers, producers, and editors in television, radio, print, and online media outlets is a great way to distribute your message to a wider audience. You can also distribute a press release via a news wire service such as PR Newswire, EIN Presswire, eReleases, Cision, PRWeb, or Newswire. Sending your press release to a wire service distributes your message to editorial offices and journalists across print media, industry-specific online outlets, news agencies, and media database systems.

Social Media

Social media allows brands to engage with their audience while also providing information on their products, services, and values. Used well, it can be a fabulous PR tool. From Twitter (now X) to Instagram, social media has rapidly become a valuable method

---

7 "Sign up for free media coverage," Source of Sources, accessed December 5, 2024, https://sourceofsources.com/.

for consumers to research a brand before it is even aware of the buyer's interest. Potential customers find social proof through customers who have already interacted with brands on social media channels. Additionally, brands can make themselves appear more human as they engage with their audience.

Blogging

Blogging is a powerful marketing tool that increases website traffic, promotes products and services, and builds customer trust. A high-quality blog with useful and engaging content can differentiate your company from its competitors by creating relevant content for your target audience. Blogs are clear and accurate, easy to share or reference, and achieve specific goals. Consider implementing a blog on your website. High-quality blogs generate content on a frequent basis. They answer questions, solve problems, entertain, and provide potential customers with information.

Search Engine Optimization

SEO generates traffic from free, organic, editorial, or natural search results through search engines. It aims to improve your website's position in search results pages. Some helpful SEO tips and tools include optimizing your site's existing content with keywords, appropriate graphics, and relevant, timely, and pertinent information. Update your content on a regular basis.

Industry Trade Shows, Webinars, and Seminars

Trade shows, seminars, and webinars are great tools to address issues, generate leads, and introduce a new product or service. Trade shows are industry-specific events that give consumers the opportunity to meet with brand representatives face-to-face, which provides a more personable experience. Seminars and webinars can also establish your brand as a thought leader in your industry, giving consumers an easy outlet to learn about your company, product, or service. These online or in-person events can be informational events to inform potential customers about the benefits of your products and services.

Depending on timing and budgets, most companies will execute a combination of the communication strategies and tools listed above.

Intuition

"Know what sparks the light in you so that you, in your own way, can illuminate the world." – Oprah Winfrey

Just as the sixth chakra, the third eye chakra, correlates with intuition, truth, and knowingness, the sixth marketing center invites us to reflect and pause to determine what is working and what is not. By now, we've developed a strong core (database) and research, created the product or service offering, and created and implemented marketing processes and procedures that include various communications strategies and tactics.

In our ever-changing business environment, where digital strategy, overflowing inboxes, data, analytics, and algorithms often take center stage, there's a subtle but often-overlooked force at work. Marketers and business professionals may focus on the more strategic and practical approach to conducting business, following methods that have been tried and validated; yet something operating at a deeper level has the power to create maximum results. Today, this subtle energetic force is reshaping the way we approach marketing and business in general.

And what is this energetic force? Intuition.

Embracing intuition in marketing is not just a trend; it's a transformative journey that transcends old paradigms and boundaries. As well as using analytics and sales to determine whether our strategies and tactics are working, we also rely on direct feedback from our customers. Engaging with ourselves and our customers is a matter of relationship, and like any relationship, it draws upon intuition for effective communication.

Evaluating Results

To determine whether it is prudent to maintain current strategies and tactics or change them, we rely on customer feedback, analytics, and sales, which includes the return on investment (ROI). I recently worked with a client who had spent $5,000.00 on social media advertising and, in return, did not receive one new client or lead.

To establish a new way forward, I asked the client to reevaluate where their customers were working and playing online. After a bit of research and some flat-out soul searching and intuitive reflection, the client admitted that most of their target client base was older and not on social media at all. We revamped their marketing strategy. Diverting funds from social media, they began to focus on Google advertising. This approach promoted their services on Google's search engine, YouTube, and other affiliated websites. By using Google Ads, the client was able to capture a significant volume of unbranded search traffic that they couldn't reach on social media. This strategy allowed them to introduce their brand to a wide audience of potential customers, driving awareness and consideration for their services.

Another area where intuition comes into play is timing.

Case Study: Be Aware of Opportunities

In October of 2012, I promoted the release of Patricia Selbert's debut autobiographical novel, *The House of Six Doors. Kirkus Reviews* said of the book, "Selbert's debut novel chronicles an immigrant's journey from the Dutch Caribbean island of Curaçao to Hollywood in the '70s. An engaging, sincere, and powerful account of an immigrant family chasing the American dream."

One of my encounters with Patricia and her book holds a fond place in my memory banks. It was just a good example of the world of PR and the sometimes stressful, often adventurous, and occasionally unexpected journey of a publicist.

Upon the release of Patricia's first book, *The House of Six Doors*, she had planned a book launch party for family and friends. Being an incredibly gracious human being, Patricia invited me to stay at her beach house in the quaint surfing town of Carpinteria, just south of Santa Barbara, over the course of the book launch weekend.

I did my due diligence for the book launch, including executing a robust marketing and PR campaign at least six months ahead of time. Despite my focused best efforts and the author's well-written and poignant book, I had no results leading up to the launch.

A mere couple of hours before the book launch event, I was still distributing press releases and pitches, working for earned media coverage and media interest in Patricia's book.

"I give up, God. I've done the best I can do." I said to myself.

Within moments, my phone rang. It was a professional and well-respected journalist who said that he would accompany me to the book launch event.

As God would have it, my new journalist friend was indeed someone special. He was, in fact, an experienced investigative journalist, Michael Bowker. He has written eleven *Lifetime* movies, numerous stories for *Reader's Digest,* the *Los Angeles Times,* and a plethora of other media outlets. He's written speeches for governors and published books with Simon & Schuster and other publishers.

And he did, in fact, read Patricia's book and write an extensive and balanced article on it for a local publication in Santa Barbara. The story was picked up and syndicated internationally, which resulted in fantastic media coverage for the author and her brand-new book.

The book became the first runner-up in the Eric Hoffer Award for general fiction in 2011 and the first runner-up in the San Francisco Book Festival for the teen category in 2011.

Despite my earlier lack of substantial coverage and results, the outcomes came together because of our highly refined communication strategies. With one thoughtful and well-written local article, we garnered a feature story for the author and her book in *MORE Magazine.*

The most exciting news came when the author's homeland of Curaçao became an independent country, the largest Dutch Overseas Territory. We distributed a highly targeted press release and were able to secure Patricia an interview on the *BBC.* Due to her relevance as an author and expert and the good timing of the press communication, she received more airtime than the country's prime minister.

The Rule of Seven

Continued relationship development with our customers is one of the most important communication strategies to maintain. The practice requires significant devotion and attention. An old adage in marketing called *The Rule of Seven* says that a prospect needs to "hear" an advertiser's message seven times before they will take action. Of course, intuition plays a role in determining where consumers are hearing the message and how and when to best communicate again. So, how do you maintain such continual communication?

There are a variety of ways. For example, you are preparing to launch a new product or service and would like to communicate the news to your customers, clients, vendors, and prospective buyers. Start by clearly communicating the information with your staff and employees. This could happen during an all-hands meeting, via an internal company newsletter, a podcast, or through simple email correspondence.

Once the team is informed, you'll want to communicate the launch externally via a PR tool such as a one-page press release distributed to local, regional, and national media. You'll also want to communicate the exciting news to your customers, clients, buyers, and prospective buyers so that you can spread your message far and wide. You might consider using an external newsletter distributed via Constant Contact, MailChimp or Flodesk. You may also choose to communicate via advertising or a specific price promotional campaign.

Even when you are not launching a new product or service, reaching out to your database on a monthly or quarterly basis is a sound marketing strategy. Whether it's a holiday card, blog update, new-hire announcement, digital newsletter, or E-Zine, keeping customers up to date on your company, employees, and projects is a good way to keep your product or service at the forefront of your audience's awareness.

Rather than constantly bombarding your email list, meaningful and well-timed communications with vital information can be planned effectively up to a year or more in advance of deployment via an editorial calendar.

Informed intuition uses the scientific elements of marketing, including data-backed insights, to help inform the artistic, or often gut-driven, more intuitive elements of marketing. With the effective use of that data, you can begin to see the success of your marketing skyrocket.

Wisdom

"Don't ask yourself what the world needs. Ask yourself what makes you come alive, and go do that, because what the world needs is people who have come alive." – Howard Thurman

In yoga, the seventh chakra correlates with wisdom, and so the final marketing center is where we use our wisdom to evaluate what's thriving and figure out how to duplicate that success. This is where I like to incorporate Pareto's Principle—or the 80/20 rule—into the marketing process.

Vilfredo Pareto was an Italian economist who observed in 1906 that 80 percent of the land in Italy was owned by 20 percent of the population. He later observed that 20 percent of the pea pods in his garden contained 80 percent of the peas.[8]

---

8 "The story of Vilfredo Pareto and the 80/20 Principle," Talent Stream, accessed September 13, 2024, https://www.talentstream.co.za/pareto-80-20-principle/.

In marketing, the premise is that 80 percent of profits come from 20 percent of customers. Another way of thinking of this is that 80 percent of sales come from 20 percent of the products and/or services a business offers. It has been my experience that if we can determine what's working very well, we can figure out how to maintain and grow those practices, processes, and procedures.

Case Study: Build on What is Working

One of my clients, Dr. Sharon Lamm-Hartman, and her company, Inside Out Learning, are a shining example of how to build on what is working for success. Inside Out Learning provides transformative learning programs that identify and change behaviors in professionals and leaders, teams, and organizations so they can achieve exceptional results. The company offers executive coaching, communication/influencing skills, presentation skills, and mobile application pathways.

When the COVID-19 pandemic emerged in the world in 2020, Dr. Sharon and Inside Out Learning chose to dramatically shift their business from a mostly in-person consulting business to moving significant interactions to an online workspace for that time period. Her company now helps leaders and organizations learn the tools to navigate the virtual workplace. Their proprietary modules help clients shine online, establish trust, master new technologies, improve communication, and build relationships. As a result, their clients and their businesses stand out as competent, technology-savvy groups of professionals.

For Dr. Sharon, we implemented a varied national, regional, and local PR campaign to brand her as a highly professional expert in her field. Given her strong credentials, including a PhD from Columbia University and twenty-five years of global experience, this was a natural alignment.

We managed to get coverage for Dr. Sharon and her team in *The Arizona Republic, Forbes Magazine, Oprah Magazine, The New York Times, Authority Magazine, Redbook Magazine, Thrive Global, Yahoo! Finance,* and *Sonoran Living on ABC15.*

Understand Your Clientele and Their Needs

At its core, marketing wisdom is about understanding your clientele and their needs. It is about being able to put yourself in their shoes and expect what they want or need to obtain from your product or service.

Knowledge is about facts, which we learn from research, education, observation, and experience. Wisdom is the ability to discern and judge which aspects of that knowledge are positively applicable to your life and work experiences. One might say that it is the prudent application of knowledge that defines wisdom. And that prudence comes from knowing the meaning or reason for knowledge and what it means to you.

The Yoga *of* Life

Approaching life from a yogic mindset, building and marketing your business with energy and the chakras in mind, and meditating and balancing your chakras, impacts more than just you or your business. As you will see in Rachel Sacco's chapter, "The Yoga of Leadership," she blazed new territory as a female CEO by influencing the people she leads, which has a positive impact on a community.

Rachel is the President and CEO of Experience Scottsdale, a world-class tourism organization based in Scottsdale, Arizona. A respected leader in the community as well as a dear friend, Rachel shares her story about integrating the benefits of mindfulness into a leadership context in a way that inspires and empowers.

4

The Yoga of Leadership

BY RACHEL SACCO

"A leader is one who knows the way, goes the way, and shows the way." – John C. Maxwell

I have been in the destination business for almost forty years, and it hasn't been easy. In fact, it was downright energy-sapping at times, yet I wanted and believed it was possible to have it all—a workplace where I could be my best self, working at a job that I loved, while having time for the family I adored. But the harder I strived to achieve the perfect balance, the worse I felt.

Oddly enough, the resolution to that journey was informed by yoga.

But let's start at the beginning of my story. In the seventies and eighties, there were very few role models for women who worked outside the home. If you grew up during the same time and you were lucky, as I was, you had a mother who instilled in you the values of integrity, compassion, hard work, and organization. But even then, if your mother was like mine, she probably taught you by example. Much of her life was about sacrifice and putting others first. And often, she stood down to avoid conflict.

Back then, we were not taught how to claim our power. We were not empowered to become all that we could be. We had yet to learn the meaning of "lean in," as Sheryl Sandberg described in her book by that title.[9] We were only just beginning to feel the magnetic pull of that boardroom table. We were only just beginning to know that it was not only our right, but our responsibility, to have a seat at that table, and once seated, to lean in, contribute, and lead—and to lead in a different way than our male counterparts. Unfortunately, that unfolding knowledge fit uneasily with the traditional roles we were still expected to fill.

Like many women of that time, I did not have a mentor. There was no one to show me how to balance the new with the old. Most of what I learned about leading, I learned by making mistakes. Most of the women I worked with in the eighties emulated the only role models available at that time, all of whom were men. I mistakenly thought that strength came in a suit with a loud voice and that kindness was a weakness. I made the mistake of thinking that letting my guard down to reveal my humanness was unprofessional. So, in the beginning, I was a terrible manager. The more I tried to control everyone and everything around me, to be absolutely perfect at everything I did, the more I made myself—and my team—miserable. In the effort to "fit in," I wasn't being true to myself.

Everything came to a head for me in 1988 when I was in the hospital and about to give birth to my first child, my son. As the first department head at my small company to go on maternity leave, no protocols were in place. I gave birth at 4:30 a.m. At

---

9 Sheryl Sandburg, *Lean In: Women, Work, and the Will to Lead* (Knopf, 2013).

11:00 a.m. that same day, I had co-workers come to the hospital so that I could review and approve an advertising campaign.

Of course, I took the standard twelve-week maternity leave, but I still came into the office for every staff meeting and worked from home every day. Mail and files were delivered to me at least three times a week, often daily. (We had no computers then, remember!) I would call into the office daily, and I maintained the responsibility of selling advertising for our first cooperative advertising piece.

Amidst all that, I was told to enjoy my time off with my newborn baby!

I don't want you to misunderstand; I worked with good people, and I worked for a great organization. My point is this: there were no blueprints for how to approach maternity leave at that time. Not for me, not for the organization. As a new mom, with no clue about how to set boundaries for work expectations, my anxiety rose. I couldn't relinquish the sense that I had to do it all. While I was on maternity leave, I often woke up in the middle of the night—as early as two or three a.m.—so that I could work until my baby awoke around five. That way, I could spend time with him before the daily packets arrived.

I continued this approach for my second and third children. By then, I was exhausted, physically and emotionally. One day, I just broke. My heart felt like an eggshell that had cracked open. Everything inside me was raw and exposed, all my flaws on display for everyone to see. Everyone around me knew as well as I did that I was failing at the two things I wanted to excel at most: motherhood and my job.

But being broken turned out to be a blessing in disguise, because it changed the course of my life for the better. Once I had broken open, I knew I had to change my life. I knew I *wanted* to change my life. I began to wonder when I had last felt truly at peace. And guess what? That's where yoga comes in. I had last felt truly at peace during a yoga class. I recalled feeling centered and calm as I had stretched my body, breathing deeply, letting my thoughts slow down.

Longing to replicate that feeling, I began doing yoga a few minutes each day. Off the mat, I reminded myself to breathe deeply, to really *feel* my feelings, and to meditate whenever I felt anxious or stressed, even for a couple of minutes.

With yogic principles as the basis for a fresh start, I kept the same job, but I began creating a work environment for my team that reflected the kind of environment I wanted to work in myself. I created a space that my team and I could look forward to entering each day, where we felt valued and inspired to do our best work.

That environment inspired me to get real and stop pretending to be someone else. I stopped emulating the men I had worked for and instead became myself. A woman. A strong woman with a kind heart. I merged the person I was at home with the person I was at work. Instead of pretending I had it all figured out, I began being honest about what I needed, where I was struggling, and when I needed help. And I started practicing the word "no," rather than saying "yes" to anything and everything.

Soon, others around me began doing the same—and not just members of my team. Other people in the same organization followed suit. It was almost a revolution. And you know what? I didn't fail. The organization didn't fail. The departments didn't fall apart. Instead, we became more closely linked as a team, more synchronized, and more productive. Our growing sense of trust and openness branched out into the community and the industry I worked in, which led to a new spirit of collaboration amongst our organization and the businesses we represented.

We were in flow. I realized that I was not only the CEO of my company but also of my life, and I taught others to be the CEOs of their lives.

If I were to write the letters CEO on a whiteboard, the familiar corresponding words—chief executive officer—impart no compelling meaning. But consider other possible definitions for that acronym:

C = Creative, Caring, Compassionate, Confident, Catalyst.
E = Enthusiastic, Encouraging, Effective, Engaging.
O = Officer, Openness, Opportunity, Organization.

These words embody the central principles of yoga. They resonated with me much more than *chief executive officer*, and they also resonated with my team. Our greatest success began the moment we embraced them. Together, we developed one of the most successful destination brands in the country: Scottsdale, Arizona. And I am proud to say that we are one of the most respected organizations in our field.

In true yogic fashion, I learned that everything I need is right inside me, sitting quietly in my own heart. An inner guide tells me all I need to do and all I need to know. The more real, open, and vulnerable I am, the more I can connect with other people and make better decisions.

I discovered the quiet power of leading by example, of listening more than speaking, of sharing more than talking. I learned that the best way to lead is with kindness. Kindness lifts others up and shows them they are valued. It kindles respect, which inspires trust, and that creates great results.

I tell every single candidate I interview and every employee I hire, from the mailroom to the vice president and everyone in between, that I expect them to operate as if they were the CEO of their own area. Their response to that statement tells me a lot about them. It tells me where they may need coaching. It tells me where they may have lacked support in the past. It also tells me about their worldview of the world, whether they are operating from love or fear. (Or, as my meditation teacher might say, whether they operate from *yum* or *yuck*.)

By getting to know my staff at a more personal level, I can help them become the CEOs not only of their work area but also of their own lives.

Do you know the kind of life *you* want to live? Not the one that you think you should have, or the one that your husband or family thinks you're supposed to have, but the one that you actually want. Let go of who you think you are *supposed* to be and embrace who you *really are*—your true and authentic self—because that is when your true inner CEO will come shining through.

And if you don't like the story of your life so far, change it. If I can do it, you can too. After all, you are the CEO of your own story. You are the CEO of your own life. And no one can change your story's ending but you. So let go of cultural and societal expectations. Follow the storyline of your heart, which is written by your intuition. As you begin to do this, you will serendipitously meet helpers along the way who add wisdom and grace to your life. They may stand in your way or open doors, but if you open your heart to those encounters, you will find healing and growth.

Reflect on the fresh definitions of that CEO title because you are a CEO. It is not just your right; it is your destiny to lean into that part of your story.

Our journey to joy, acceptance, wholeness, gratitude, and peace is how we as leaders change the world. One story at a time, one serendipitous encounter at a time, one CEO—Caring Enormously for Others—at a time.

Mindful Leader Exercise

The research on meditation and mindfulness is clear: these internal practices reap external success. To destress, balance your personal and professional lives, and build your leadership capacity, incorporate the following practices into your life.

1. **Breathe.** This sounds so simple, yet most of us hold our breath during moments of stress. When overwhelm strikes, pause and take five deep breaths. Deep breathing, sometimes called diaphragmatic breathing, enables more air to flow into the body, which helps calm nerves and reduce anxiety and stress.
2. **Be compassionate with yourself and others.** Compassion is a big part of mindful leadership. By listening more and talking less, compassionate leaders are better able to connect with and empower team members. This helps your team feel cared for, seen, heard, and understood.
3. **Become self-aware.** As Socrates said, "Know Thyself." True wisdom is knowing what you do not know. So, an essential part of knowing yourself is recognizing the limits of your own wisdom and understanding—knowing what you do genuinely and recognizing what you have yet to learn.
4. **Become accountable.** Mindful leaders are accountable for their team's failures, not just their successes. They promote a culture of individual accountability and convert mistakes into learning and growth opportunities.
5. **Hold regular and intentional meditation and mindfulness sessions.** Create a quiet or silent space where employees can go to sit or work without any distractions. As Steve

> Jobs once said about meditation, "You start to see things more clearly and be in the present more. Your mind just slows down, and you see a tremendous expanse at the moment. You see so much more than you could see before."

Employing these principles will help you embrace who you *really are*—your true and authentic self—and in doing so lead others to do the same.

5

The Yoga of Life

"Magic is believing in yourself, if you can do that, you can make anything happen." – Johann Wolfgang von Goethe

I sincerely hope that you are well on your way to living a more conscious, mindful, and aware life. My thoughts on yoga and marketing are just a tiny glimpse into my own journey, which has certainly been one of ups and downs, blessings and sorrows, and everything in between.

It's my hope that you will become committed to a peace-centered life and join me as we all learn more about consciousness, mindfulness, and awareness, and how these concepts underlie all of the good things in life, like faith, hope, and love.

Here are some of the tools I recommend to help you get started with your mindfulness journey or help it grow.

Start Meditating!

As you begin or progress on your journey toward meditation, mindfulness, and marketing, I recommend taking a meditation class. Twenty minutes of meditation a day can have a huge positive impact on your outlook, attitude, health, and overall balanced life journey.

If you have ever tried to sit in silence for longer than a few minutes with your thoughts racing around like a monkey mind, you have realized that most normal people cannot learn sustainable meditation by themselves. Experiment with different types of meditation. The three major types include: mantra, breathing, and visualization. Not all will work for everyone, so figure out what works best for you.

My first meditation class was Primordial Sound Meditation, in which the McLean Meditation Institute and the Chopra Center for Wellbeing gave me a specific mantra to chant silently based on the date and time of my birth, which aligned with the earth's specific vibration at that time.

I recommend the McLean Meditation Institute for meditation classes and retreats.[10]

Find ways to incorporate meditation into your life.

Make Time for Meditation

If you don't commit to your meditation practice, you won't reap all the potential rewards, so make time for it. You can meditate anywhere. Even people who are extremely busy find plenty of

10 The McLean Meditation Institute, accessed December 10, 2024, https://mcleanmeditation.com.

opportunities to meditate: in the shower, while walking, during lunch, or sitting at a desk. Persistence and consistency will bring long-term benefits.

Create a Ritual

Choose a ritual to begin your routine, something you can employ even when you travel. Whether it's lighting a candle, sitting on the floor with your legs crossed, or drinking tea, what is important is that creating the ritual happens quickly, effortlessly, and simply.

Expand Your Experience Through Yoga

Mary Oliver asks the question, "What is it that you will do with your one wild and precious life?"

What were you born to do? What are your unique talents and gifts?

Sooner or later, in almost everyone's life, the soul comes knocking. It takes time, present-moment awareness, and mindfulness to hear the universal whispers answering these questions. Eventually, you will discover your *Swadharma*, a Sanskrit word that means "your own life purpose according to your nature." Another word for this concept is *Dharma,* meaning a person's highest purpose in life.

According to Indian philosophy, yoga is the system of gaining knowledge through direct experience. How, for example, would you know what a peach tastes like unless you actually eat one?

Yoga's goal is to help us connect the body, mind, and spirit and to build strength, flexibility, and balance. By integrating the physical, mental, and spiritual aspects of who we are as human beings, we can begin to understand the workings of the body and mind.

Transcending the mind through meditation allows us to directly experience our essential, authentic selves, the spiritual core that lies within us all. This space of sacred consciousness is where anything is possible, and there are infinite possibilities in life.

Mindful Seeing Exercise

This simple exercise helps promote a feeling of peace and interconnectedness.

1. Find a space at a window with some kind of view where there are sights to be seen outside.
2. Look at everything there is to see. Avoid labeling and categorizing what you see outside the window. Instead of thinking "squirrel" or "tree," simply notice the colors, textures, and patterns of energy.
3. Pay attention to the movement of leaves or the grass in the breeze. Notice the many different shapes in everything you see. Try to see the world outside the window from the perspective of someone unfamiliar with these sights. It is sometimes called the beginner's mind.
4. Be observant but not judgmental or critical. Be aware but not fixated.
5. If you become distracted, bring your gaze right back to the present moment.

You can do the same exercise but switch it to "Mindful Listening."

Find Your Agent of Change Within

Shortly after I learned to meditate, I wrote an article for the 2007 issue of *Desert Living Magazine* entitled *There's No Place Like OM.*[11] That article became an early inspiration for *There's No Place Like OM,* a documentary film series I am currently producing with Pronoia Productions.[12] That article follows. Some aspects of the piece may sound counterintuitive, but the more you immerse yourself in yogic practices and balance your seven chakras, the sooner you'll begin on your journey to mindfulness.

Sometimes the best place to find an agent of change is within. And you get there by simply doing nothing.

> *If you think meditation is just for chanting monks or new age hippies, think again. This practice, whose DNA is derived from ancient spiritual practice, has gone mainstream. Meditation is now attracting on-the-go urban socialites, celebrities, and maybe even your neighbor. Growing in popularity, everyone from the Mayo Clinic to Jennifer Aniston is singing its praises (or chanting its OMs). Some use it to discover health and happiness, while others say it helps their careers. Corporations, such as Marriott and*

11

12 "There's No Place Like OM," Trailer, Pronoia Productions, accessed September 14, 2024, http://www.pronoia.tv/current-project.html.

Hilton, use it in stress-relief programs, while NASA even incorporates it to keep their employees productive and help them become better leaders.

Although there are no hard numbers on how many Americans meditate, the National Institute of Health spends over $10 million annually on meditation research. There's even a course called "Meditation for Millionaires" offered at a posh Florida resort.

The jury is in for Judge Roland Steinle III, a retired Superior Court Judge in Maricopa County. "I got into it when my cardiologist told me to reduce my stress," he says. "Since I started, I am calmer in a chaotic world, and I sleep better. Soon I will go to a meditation retreat and take it to the next level."

An architect in Fountain Hills, Arizona agrees: "Practicing meditation allows me to better access my innate creativity as it applies to my own health and wellness," says Thomas Bohlen of Oracle Architecture and Planning. "It also helps me make better business decisions."

Our writer heads to a chic desert retreat looking for high thread counts but finds luxury of another sort—one of inner peace.

I had been to retreats before—some for renewal, some for relaxation, others for detox. But none helped me reconnect with my inner peace and discover a new enthusiasm that would inspire and sustain me for so long as this one—a retreat focused on the practice of meditation.

Everyone in our group of about fifteen came with his or her own idea of what the weekend would hold. I wanted

> *R&R and the Eat, Pray, Love experience crammed into 48 hours. One came to get away from her teenagers; another came to find balance; and a couple came because they were moving to Sedona.*
>
> *I expected to deepen and enhance my meditation practice and spiritual connection in the perfect red rock setting. However, I didn't know that going for three days without meat or junk food would be part of this process. (All of the food featured at the retreat was vegetarian, organic, and prepared by Ayurvedic chefs.) With our daily addictions fighting a slow death, a group of us had a mini-breakdown in our hotel room and devoured an entire bag of Cheetos and a bottle of wine, but the next morning we got up bright and early and were back on the mat, downward-facing dogging.*
>
> *In addition to reviving my meditation practice, I engaged in several mindfulness exercises. Each experience was designed to heighten the senses, from hikes through the Coconino Forest and vortexes to quiet journaling exercises, I increased my awareness and learned how to bring balance into my life.*
>
> *I'd heard it before, but it finally made sense to me. When you learn to appreciate the moment you're in, rather than worrying about the past or future, life gets better. When I returned home, my husband was happy I'd found my chi (even though I reeked of curry).*

I sincerely hope that this book has provided you with some fundamentals of the vast world of yoga, mindfulness, meditation, the chakras, and how the benefits derived from incorporating these ancient yet now mainstream practices into your life can positively impact your business and marketing. As everything is the continual swirling of information and energy, by becoming part of the conscious, mindfulness, and yoga community, we can participate in this dynamic dance of the universe.

You do not need to leave your room. Remain sitting at your table and listen. Do not even listen; simply wait, and be quiet, still, and solitary. The world will freely offer itself to you to be unmasked; it has no choice; it will roll in ecstasy at your feet. – Franz Kafka

The Guest House

By Rumi

This being human is a guest house.
Every morning a new arrival.
A joy, a depression, a meanness
Some momentary awareness comes
as an unexpected visitor.
Welcome and entertain them all!
Even if they're a crowd of sorrows,
Who violently sweep your house
empty of its furniture,
still, treat each guest honorably.
He may be clearing you out
for some new delight.
The dark thought, the shame, the malice,
meet them at the door laughing,
and invite them in.
Be grateful for whoever comes,
because each has been sent
as a guide from beyond.

Acknowledgements

I offer my heartfelt and sincere gratitude to everyone who helped me turn my idea of this book into reality. I am especially grateful for my wise son, Daniel, who is the light of my life; my husband, Mark, who never stops believing in me; and Michael Zelin, who is the most extraordinary father to our son.

I am blessed by and extremely grateful for my family and heart and soulful friends including my brother Steve, nephew Jeremy, Diana Ford, Liz Garlieb, Roland Steinle, Anissa and Chris Klenzman, Yvonne and Brad Kappes, Karie Fisher, Donna Armstrong, Kim Staber, Rob Ford, Mary Beth Preece, Deanna Colberg, Susan Kricun, and Trudy Reeves.

To my beautiful friend and meditation teacher, Sarah McLean, author of *Soul-Centered: Transform Your Life in 8 Weeks with Meditation and The Power of Attention*, and Marty Birrittella, author of *Field of Love: How to Experience the Field and Field of Love: Power, Love and Fortune on the Road to Enlightenment* and *Field of Love: Without This Thought…Who Am I?;* Victoria and

Peter Nelson, Joe and Rachel Sacco, Dennis Harness, Ph.D., author of *The Nakshatras: The Lunar Mansions of Vedic Astrology* and *The Karmic Code*

I'm sending sincere gratitude to Paul and Tina Bakalis, Peggy Reinhardt, Nancy Marriott, Nancy Black and Isaac Hernandez, authors of *Difference Makers: Portraits of Leaders in the Arts, Social Justice and Sustainability;* Laura Pitari, JD Messinger, author of *11 Days in May: The Conversation That Will Change Your Life* and *The 12 Habits of Authentic People;* Dennis Andres, author of *Sedona's Top 10 Hikes, Sedona: The Essential Guide, What Is a Vortex: A Practical Guide, The Insider's Guide to Sedona, What Is a Vortex?* and *Sedona Hikes 225 Trails & Loops*; Rosanne Rusnock, Feng Shui extraordinaire; and Michael Bowker, CEO of Sixty Degrees Publishing.

And to my grounded and true children by marriage, Jana and Randy, and their sweet children, Hallie Grace and young Drew.

To Debbie Tackett Haertzen, Terry Barney, and Sherrie Tackett, my early coaches. Thank you.

To my brilliant editor, Deborah Froese, I now know why the book took so many years to manifest. The book and I were waiting for you to show up in our lives. Thank you for your patience, attention to detail, grace, and commitment to the real heart of yoga, which you embody in your very presence.

Special thanks to Georgette Green and Bobby Dunaway at Indigo River for taking a chance on me and believing in my abilities. Thanks to Emma Elzinga and Freya Murphy for their design and marketing brilliance. And to Ivan Misner for selflessly connecting me with Indigo River Publishing after we met at that fabulous Jack Canfield Mastermind Retreat at Miramar by the sea in Santa Barbara.

My heartfelt gratitude goes to the marvelous mothers who hold me up and encourage me often, even though they may not know it: Tina Newman and Amy Stib. To Dr. Libby Hart-Wells, who is the embodiment of pure grace and who never tired of my mom questions. Libby, I so appreciate your advice to "give it some grace" and your constant listening ear. Thank you. And your commitment to children, students, and education is awe-inspiring. Please continue the wonderful work you are doing in the world and now at Johns Hopkins University!

To my collaboration team: Lindsay Klenzman and Megan Goodwin. Your creativity, loyalty, and commitment are abundant and unwavering. You are our future leaders. Never forget your intelligence and worth.

Many thanks to my clients past and present, who continue to inspire me and add so much light to the world including: Valerie Fitzgerald, author of *Heart & Sold: How to Survive and Thrive in Real Estate*, Colette Baron-Reid, author of *The Oracle Card Journal: A Daily Practice for Igniting Your Intuition and Magic, Oracle of the 7 Energies Journal, Messages from Spirit: Exploring Your Connection to Divine Guidance, Journey Through the Chakras, Mystical Shaman Oracle Deck and Guidebook, The Enchanted Map Oracle Cards, The Map: Finding the Magic and Meaning in the Story of Your Life, Messages from Spirit: The Extraordinary Power of Oracles, Omens and Signs, The Good Tarot, The Wisdom of Avalon Oracle Cards, Uncharted: The Journey Through Uncertainty to Infinite Possibility, Weight Loss for People Who Feel Too Much,* and *Remembering the Future: The Path to Recovering Intuition;* Jude Bijou, author of *Attitude Reconstruction: A Blueprint for Building a Better Life*, Patricia Selbert, author of *The House of Six Doors*, Dr. Sharon Lamm-Hartman, author of *The Authenticity Code: The Art of*

Success and Why You Can't Fake It to Make It, Diana Raab, author of *Writing for Bliss: A Seven-Step Plan for Telling Your Story and Transforming Your Life, Writing For Bliss: A Companion Journal, Healing with Words: A Writer's Cancer Journey, Regina's Closet: Finding my Grandmother's Secret Journal, Writers and Their Notebooks, Writers on the Edge: 22 Writers Speak About Addiction and Dependency, Getting Pregnant & Staying Pregnant: Overcoming Infertility and Managing Your High-Risk Pregnancy, An Imaginary Affair: Poems Whispered to Neruda, Lust, Listening To Africa, The Guilt Gene, Dear Anais: My Life In Poems For You*, and *My Muse Undress Me*. Richard Polak, author of *Work Smart Now: How to Jump Start Productivity, Empower Employees, and Achieve More,* and Victoria Sol, author of *Lifting the Layers to Vibrant Health: Detox for Body, Mind and Spirit.*

Thank you to the leaders, consultants, modern-day mystics, healers, yoga teachers, spiritual advisors and other extraordinary humans who have transcended the ego and are doing important energetic and healing work on our planet right now. They include: Dr. Lisa Miller, Marie Manuchehri, Phyllis Mitz, Susan Miller, Seane Corn, Caroline Myss, Maria Camille, Carissa Schumacher, Rich Moser, Brent BecVar, M.S., Allison DuBois, Danielle Gibbons, Dhargya Lobsang, Yogi Cameron, Diane Goldner, Chris Meredith, Tom McMullan, Jeva Uqualla, and so many others. I honor and admire your extraordinary gifts and talents. I work hard to effectively and frequently communicate your qualities, credibility and validity to the world.

To Marlene and Jane Wells, who taught me how to write right and act right.

To my own yoga teacher, Deborah Garland, thank you for showing me the way.

A special thanks to Mariel Hemingway, who is hosting my documentary series, *There's No Place Like OM,* and graciously offers the words of introduction to this book. I'm grateful for her participation in two projects so dear to my heart.

And finally, to my readers: I am inspired by you and your commitment to finding peace, practicing yoga, balancing your hearts and minds for success, creating and sustaining heart-centered businesses through mindful marketing, and transforming your lives through consciousness, mindfulness, and awareness. I am honored that you have chosen this book to accompany you on your journey.

APPENDIX A

Marketing Strategies and Timeline for Launching Books, New Products, or Services

Although these tactics were originally created with authors in mind—and they include some author-specific tips—they are suitable for anyone who wishes to launch a new product. Timing is key to effective publicity. Plan for a six-month to one-year window to prepare a full-blown book or new product launch.

Planning well ahead of time and staying organized make it easier to stay centered and peaceful, bringing yoga principles into your marketing approach.

Six to Twelve Months Before Launch: Seek Endorsements

- Seek endorsements for your product by sending samples to top authors, celebrities, and experts in related fields. Personalize each cover letter and let the recipient know why they should be interested in what you are offering. A positive endorsement is a great addition to the front or back cover copy of a book or on the testimonial page for a product and press materials.

- If you're an author, submit your book to *Publishers Weekly*'s announcement issue for consideration of inclusion. Many book buyers use this issue of *Publishers Weekly* as an ordering guide for the season. Other book trade publications such as *Choice, Booklist, Kirkus Reviews,* and *Library Journal* have special features and announcement issues throughout the year as well.
- Compile a list of any personal media contacts and possible review outlets for the book or product. Be sure to include local, regional, and national newspapers. Be sure to include book trade publications and book review editors at daily newspapers, high-profile radio and TV show producers, and general interest magazines in your mailing. If you are promoting a product, ensure it is going to a specific target market with interest in what your product has to offer.
- Order product samples, or for a book, galleys, or advance readers' copies (ARCs). Base your order numbers on how many reviewers you feel you will need to send a sample to. (Galleys and ARCs are both versions of bound, uncorrected proofs. Galleys, however, have plain paper covers, while ARCs have cover designs that match the final books.)

Four to Five Months Before Launch: Seek Publicity

- Outline your publicity initiatives and brainstorm pitches and angles. Before you send out product samples to the media, determine your target audiences and how to position your product. Some products or services have multiple angles. Brainstorm with your team and get creative. There are likely to be numerous types of media that could be interested in what you're offering.

- Create a press kit including a press release with photos, a brief product story, or short and long author biographies for authors and their books. It's now time to send out those samples, and you'll need promotional materials to accompany them. Your press kit should inspire an editor, writer, or producer to feature your book or product or run your piece directly as submitted. Consider including a handwritten note.
- Your submission should include a cover letter that ties your product or book to current events or emerging trends. Be sure to mention if there are plans for a tour, national advertising, or PR campaign. Position yourself as a media-trained expert. Take this opportunity to tell the media contact why *your* offering is special and newsworthy.
- Distribute your press release to top national and international media contacts. Include a request form for a sample of the product or a review copy of your book. I use the Cision media database, PR Newswire, and PR Web. There are many other media databases available as well.
- If you are sending out galleys or ARCs, make sure to check book trade publications for their specific submission guidelines. Some prefer to receive two galleys, while others only accept finished copies. Your best chance for a review is to follow their instructions. Create a targeted media list based on keywords, geography, genre, market

niches, and other unique aspects of your offering. The list you build should directly reflect the brainstorming you've just completed.

- Mail galleys, ARCs, or sample products to long-lead magazines and select top national and international media outlets. You've already created your media lists and press materials, so simply personalize your cover letters and send out your remaining galleys or sample products. Be sure to keep track of who receives samples and what angle you pitched them.

Three to Four Months Before Launch: Follow Up on Previous Outreach

- Follow up with long-lead magazines. Depending on your shipping method, you should follow up with long-lead media about two to three weeks after you send samples. If you check in earlier, they will simply tell you they haven't had a chance to look at the sample, and if you wait until later, you may find the critical connections mentioned in your press release and cover letter may no longer be relevant.
- Follow up with people who agreed to provide endorsements.
- Create a website and social media channels, including a YouTube channel. Websites and social media channels can be great promotional tools, especially if you have the time and skill to build one on your own. Update your sites frequently with new information, review quotes, and blog posts.

- Create banner ads and other graphical assets for Amazon and other online locations, such as Google. Authors can also use Goodreads, Publisher's Weekly, and so on.

Two to Three Months Before Launch: Contact Serial Publications

- Contact serial publications such as daily and weekly newspapers, weekly magazines, and regional publications via phone, email, and press releases.
- Contact news syndicates and high-profile online news sources via email and press release distribution as well as customized, targeted pitches.
- Distribute products or finished copies of the book to trade outlets and continue to follow up for long-lead magazines.
- Follow up with anyone you have already sent sample products or review copies to.
- Plan any online and in-person launch and book signing events.

One to Two Months Before Launch: Pitch to National and Syndicated Media

- Pitch the product and interviews to national and syndicated radio and television if appropriate.
- Pitch lower-profile online news sources and niche online sites.

- Follow up with news syndicates and high-profile online news sources.

One Month Before Publication: Follow Up

- Follow up with national and syndicated radio and television pitches.
- Pitch the product and interviews to local radio and local television if appropriate.
- Follow up with daily and weekly newspapers, weekly magazines, and regional publications.

Launch and Post-Launch: Keep Promoting!

- Continue to follow up, fulfill review requests for samples, and request tear sheets (copies of the article) from the media—literally, the page with your product review torn out of the newspaper or magazine.
- Follow up with local radio and local television if appropriate.
- Follow up with lower-profile online news sources and niche online sites.
- If you're a book author, submit twenty-word-or-less excerpts from published reviews to Amazon.com and other online retailers, including Google, Goodreads, and so on.
- Revisit your pitch if it relates to something newsworthy, such as a holiday, breaking news, or other events.

- There is no need to follow up with book trade publications as they have specific timelines and submission guidelines that you will have implemented by now.
- If you don't have the budget to send out large numbers of unsolicited samples, consider an email press release or pitch. Also, some book review editors are now open to reviewing an online, digital version of the book. Use the same topic-related strategy for approaching these reviewers, but instead of sending them the book, mail a packet with the press release and a review copy request form. Be sure to fulfill any resulting requests in a timely manner. That way, your book is sent to only those who are actively interested. You can also e-pitch the book to appropriate editors. The pitch should be short and to the point, with the most newsworthy element at the top, as most editors don't have time to read closely.
- Contact news syndicates and high-profile online news sources. Just as you did with daily newspapers, weekly magazines, and regional publications, take a few approaches to these widely read, syndicated media venues. Wire services reach newspapers that don't have time or staff to generate all news stories, and you'll save on sending samples to a small circulation newspaper. Online sites are read and frequented by so many internet surfers, you're guaranteed to reach a wide audience if you can land a review or feature on one of them or online via PR Web.
- Pitch product and author/creator interviews to local radio and television if appropriate. This is a great way to not only build local exposure for your book or product, but it

also adds to your reel (for television) and your credibility (for both radio and television). You can use the hook of an event or the regionalism of your product or title to get the local broadcast media's attention. They're always looking for a local angle to their stories, and your book or product might be the perfect fit.

- At this point, you may have received some positive trade or magazine reviews, and you can mention them for leverage and increased credibility by quoting them in your follow up, adding them to your website, biography, blog, social media, and so on.
- Continue to send relevant publicity updates throughout the life of your product.
- When you know that a review has run, call or email your contact to request a tear sheet.

As you can see, these strategies involve establishing a pattern of contact with those who can help you promote your book or product. While this may seem repetitive, consistency—along with great strategies and a friendly presence—is critical.

Words of Wisdom

"Have giant goals and believe in them." – Jack Canfield

I've attended a few book marketing and PR conferences throughout my career. My favorite was an event held in San Diego, California, that featured bestselling Chicken Soup for the Soul author and success coach Jack Canfield. Canfield is one of my favorite authors. He sets giant goals. The first one he set for

Chicken Soup for the Soul was to sell a million and a half books in a year and a half.

During the meeting, Jack shared with us a document titled, *How to Market a Bestseller*. I have referred to this guide many times while coaching authors and other businesspeople about how to successfully plan for and release a new book or product. Of the numerous proven marketing and PR strategies and tactics available, here are my top five recommendations, always with Jack's suggestion to have giant goals and believe in them in mind.

1. Write a Great Book/Create a Great Product

Create a powerful book or product and have someone professionally design a fabulous book cover or packaging. While these may sound like simple suggestions—and they are—nailing them is key to marketing, publicizing, and selling your book, product, or service. So many times, authors send me books that must go back to the drawing board because the cover design and internal layout do not look professional. Invest the time and money early on to get these basic things right. I have resources available if you need them.

2. Set Big Goals

Before you begin planning, do as Jack Canfield did. Set big goals so your planning will elevate to meet them.

3. Plan Ahead.

At the very least, take six months to one year to plan and implement a strategic marketing and PR campaign, like the approach described in the first part of this appendix. During this period, create relevant messaging and support materials and at least seven different story ideas, hooks, and product pitches. See what others are doing with market-related products. Gather Amazon keywords and keywords for SEO.

Make sure your press kit provides a complete yet concise overview of your book or product and its unique features and benefits. For products, include customer testimonials. For books, a quote from the author, a blurb from the publisher, and a short author bio will do. Make sure the document meets the Associated Press (AP) style. Distribute the release through a respected media database, PR Newswire, and online.

Submit your product sample to hundreds of print and broadcast reviewers. This takes time. Include a one-pager about the product and a handwritten note to the correct contact at the target publications or media outlets. Many book reviewers have stringent submission guidelines that must be followed to the letter.

4. Coordinate Amazon Promotions.

For books, this involves having a database of colleagues, friends, family, and industry associates who all buy the book during the same week for the official publication date. Ask them to include a link to the book on their websites, in their newsletters, and on their various social media channels and blogs to increase the book's rating on Amazon.

For other products, investigate utilizing seasonal sales, Amazon Prime Days, and Black Friday and Cyber Monday.

5. Establish Distribution.

Without distribution channels, you'll have a hard time getting your product into your customers' hands. While bigger companies may have these channels in place, if you are a small business or self-published author, you will have some work to do. Self-published authors will want to work with Ingram, Baker & Taylor, or the National Book Network (NBN) for distribution. One of my clients is planning to use Book Baby for distribution. A credible book distribution company may make the difference in getting your book in coveted locations such as Barnes & Noble, Costco, Target, libraries, and independent bookstores.[13]

13 This information was adapted from Jeanna Valenti's original blogpost, *Book Marketing and PR 101*, Lightbox, June 15, 2020, https://www.lightboxpr.com/2020/06/book-marketing-and-pr-101/.

APPENDIX B

Resources for Authors

Book Reviews

Book reviews help potential readers become familiar with what a book is about, give them an idea of how they might react to it, and determine whether your book will be the right book for them. Also, the presence of book reviews can help validate the worthiness of a book and establish who the book's audience is. Book reviews become essential publicity for writers. Here are some of the more prominent book reviewers. Also, most major United States newspapers have book reviewers on staff or on contract.

Goodreads
LibraryThing
Book Riot
Bookish
Booklist
Kirkus Reviews

Amazon Book Review
The Bookbag
Book Riot
IndieReader
Bookpage
The New York Review of Books
The Kindle Book Review
YouTube
Social Media
Library Journal
The New York Times Book Review
NetGalley
BookBub
Booksprout
Book Marks
Los Angeles Review of Books
The New Yorker
Chicago Review of Books
Reedsy Discovery
LoveReading
SF Book Reviews
BookSirens
Publisher's Weekly

Book Award Submissions

Winning or being nominated for a book award brings credibility and publicity, thus contributing to increased interest in your book among both consumers and booksellers. There are many book award options, including:

Benjamin Franklin Awards
Nautilus Book Awards
BookBrowse Awards
Best Book Award (American Book Fest)
Pulitzer Prize
Booker Prize
The John Newbery Award
Michael Printz Award
Edgar Awards
National Book Critics Circle Award
National Book Awards
Costa Book Awards
Women's Prize for Fiction
PEN/Bellwether Prize
Colorado Book Awards
Hollywood Book Festival
International Book Award Contest
National Indie Excellence Award
NextGen Indie Book Awards
Reader's Favorite
The National Book Awards
The Wishing Shelf
Woodson Book Award
Rubery Book Award
Foreword INDIES
Midwest Book Awards
The Moonbeam Children's Book Awards
The Royal Dragonfly Book Awards
The Golden Kite Award
Mom's Choice Award
The Purple Dragonfly Book

Christian Book Awards Contests
Illumination Awards
Christian Indie Awards
Christian Book Awards
Carol Awards
The Inspy Awards
Christianity Today Book Award
CPA Book Awards
The Christy Awards
The IndieReader Discovery Awards
The Best Indie Book Award
Foreword INDIES Book of the Year
Indie Reader Discovery Awards
The Independent Publisher Book Awards
The Eric Hoffer Award
Next Generation Indie Book Awards
The Edgar Awards
eLit Awards
Global E-Book Awards
Digital Book World Awards
Hugo Awards
Nebula Awards
Axiom Business Book Awards
Spur Awards
WILLA
American Fiction Awards

Goodreads Presence

Goodreads is the world's largest site for readers and book recommendations. It also serves as a social media community with over 85 million users and members. Goodreads giveaways effectively raise awareness for new titles, build buzz and word-of-mouth excitement through reviews, and increase visibility through their online "to-read" shelf activity.

Publishers Weekly Email Banner Ad

Publishers Weekly, also known as PW, is the leading publication serving the entire international book publishing industry. To introduce your book to the industry, I recommend designing and placing a customized banner ad in one or more issues of Publishers Weekly's PW Daily email newsletter, which is sent to more than 42,000 bookstore buyers, librarians, journalists, and other publishing industry professionals.

Contact Jeanna

To get the latest *The Yoga of Marketing* updates and resources, visit: https://theyogaofmarketing.com

Jeanna speaks frequently on the topic of marketing and mindfulness. She can deliver a keynote presentation or break-out session depending on your organization's needs. If you are interested in finding out more, please visit Jeanna at https://www.lightboxpr.com

You can also connect with Jeanna on her blog, *The Inspired Publicist,* here: https://www.lightboxpr.com/category/the-inspired-publicist/

Jeanna's online course, The Yoga of Marketing, is now available on Udemy here: https://www.udemy.com/user/jeanna-valenti

www.ingramcontent.com/pod-product-compliance
Lightning Source LLC
LaVergne TN
LVHW010920110826
845149LV00013B/2432

9781964686837